THIS IS YOUR **PASSBOOK®** FOR ...

BEGINNING OFFICE ASSISTANT

NLC®
NATIONAL LEARNING CORPORATION®
passbooks.com

NLC®

National Learning Corporation

212 Michael Drive, Syosset, NY 11791
(516) 921-8888 • www.passbooks.com
E-mail: info@passbooks.com

PUBLISHED IN THE UNITED STATES OF AMERICA

PASSBOOK® SERIES

THE *PASSBOOK® SERIES* has been created to prepare applicants and candidates for the ultimate academic battlefield – the examination room.

At some time in our lives, each and every one of us may be required to take an examination – for validation, matriculation, admission, qualification, registration, certification, or licensure.

Based on the assumption that every applicant or candidate has met the basic formal educational standards, has taken the required number of courses, and read the necessary texts, the *PASSBOOK® SERIES* furnishes the one special preparation which may assure passing with confidence, instead of failing with insecurity. Examination questions – together with answers – are furnished as the basic vehicle for study so that the mysteries of the examination and its compounding difficulties may be eliminated or diminished by a sure method.

This book is meant to help you pass your examination provided that you qualify and are serious in your objective.

The entire field is reviewed through the huge store of content information which is succinctly presented through a provocative and challenging approach – the question-and-answer method.

A climate of success is established by furnishing the correct answers at the end of each test.

You soon learn to recognize types of questions, forms of questions, and patterns of questioning. You may even begin to anticipate expected outcomes.

You perceive that many questions are repeated or adapted so that you can gain acute insights, which may enable you to score many sure points.

You learn how to confront new questions, or types of questions, and to attack them confidently and work out the correct answers.

You note objectives and emphases, and recognize pitfalls and dangers, so that you may make positive educational adjustments.

Moreover, you are kept fully informed in relation to new concepts, methods, practices, and directions in the field.

You discover that you arre actually taking the examination all the time: you are preparing for the examination by "taking" an examination, not by reading extraneous and/or supererogatory textbooks.

In short, this PASSBOOK®, used directedly, should be an important factor in helping you to pass your test.

BEGINNING OFFICE ASSISTANT

DUTIES:

As an **Office Assistant I**, you would perform entry-level clerical and office support work, including processing transactions and maintaining records, in a variety of organizational settings, to meet the requirements of agency programs. Examples of your duties may include: keeping records; retrieving and compiling information; performing basic arithmetic calculations; mail, supply, and inventory functions; some keyboarding and other document preparation tasks; answering telephones; completing forms; answering questions or otherwise assisting customers; or creating or assisting in the preparation of reports, charts, graphs, and tables.

As an **Office Assistant I (Stores and Mail),** you would spend most of your work time performing general office support and clerical duties, related to mail receipt, mail distribution, storage, and storeskeeping.

As a **Business Document Specialist Trainee**, you would perform duties similar to those performed by Office Assistants I while learning to review and approve documents and provide information related to the creation and dissolution of business entities.

As an **Employee Insurance Reviewing Clerk Trainee**, you would perform duties similar to those performed by Office Assistants I, while learning to provide information and process transactions related to health insurance programs run by the State.

As a **Licensing Services Clerk Trainee**, you would perform duties similar to those performed by Office Assistants I, while learning to review and process various types of transactions related to professional licensing. Processing these transactions may involve reading and interpreting various laws, rules, regulations, and policies. You frequently will communicate with license applicants and the public.

As a **Medicaid Eligibility Examiner Trainee**, you would perform duties similar to those performed by Office Assistants I while learning how to assist in or determine eligibility for Medicaid (or public health insurance programs), and provide technical assistance and guidance to local social services districts, other State employees, consumers, health care providers, professional organizations, insurance companies, and advocacy groups. Public contact may be frequent.

As a **Payroll Assistant Trainee**, you would perform duties similar to those performed by Office Assistants I, while learning how to prepare and process payroll transactions and review related documents; answer basic payroll questions; and provide payroll customer service to agency employees.

As a **Public Service Commission Operations Clerk Trainee**, you would perform duties similar to those performed by Office Assistants I, while learning how to perform a variety of activities with regard to processing Public Service Commission orders, notices, rulings, and tariff filings; assist agency staff and the public with researching and retrieval of public documents filed with the agency; analyze formal and informal petitions filed with the Commission; and make determinations on appropriate categories and distribution of the petitions.

SUBJECT OF EXAMINATION

The written test is designed to test for knowledge, skills, and/or abilities in such areas as:

1. **Reading** - These questions test for the ability to read and understand short written passages. You will be asked one question about each passage. Everything you need to know to answer the question is contained in the passage. You should base your answer only on the information contained in the passage, and not on what you may know about the topic.
2. **Working with others** - These questions test for knowledge of how to interact with others in a constructive, courteous, and effective manner. Questions will involve working or interacting with a variety of individuals in a variety of circumstances.
3. **Name and number checking** - These questions test for the ability to accurately check names, words, and numbers that are almost exactly alike. Information will be presented in two or three columns. You must compare entries across the columns and mark your answers in accordance with the directions given.
4. **Operations with letters and numbers** - These questions test for the ability to perform a variety of operations using letters and numbers. You must alphabetize, arrange, compare, check, and/or count given groups of letters and/or numbers, in order to answer the questions correctly.

HOW TO TAKE A TEST

I. YOU MUST PASS AN EXAMINATION

A. WHAT EVERY CANDIDATE SHOULD KNOW

Examination applicants often ask us for help in preparing for the written test. What can I study in advance? What kinds of questions will be asked? How will the test be given? How will the papers be graded?

As an applicant for a civil service examination, you may be wondering about some of these things. Our purpose here is to suggest effective methods of advance study and to describe civil service examinations.

Your chances for success on this examination can be increased if you know how to prepare. Those "pre-examination jitters" can be reduced if you know what to expect. You can even experience an adventure in good citizenship if you know why civil service exams are given.

B. WHY ARE CIVIL SERVICE EXAMINATIONS GIVEN?

Civil service examinations are important to you in two ways. As a citizen, you want public jobs filled by employees who know how to do their work. As a job seeker, you want a fair chance to compete for that job on an equal footing with other candidates. The best-known means of accomplishing this two-fold goal is the competitive examination.

Exams are widely publicized throughout the nation. They may be administered for jobs in federal, state, city, municipal, town or village governments or agencies.

Any citizen may apply, with some limitations, such as the age or residence of applicants. Your experience and education may be reviewed to see whether you meet the requirements for the particular examination. When these requirements exist, they are reasonable and applied consistently to all applicants. Thus, a competitive examination may cause you some uneasiness now, but it is your privilege and safeguard.

C. HOW ARE CIVIL SERVICE EXAMS DEVELOPED?

Examinations are carefully written by trained technicians who are specialists in the field known as "psychological measurement," in consultation with recognized authorities in the field of work that the test will cover. These experts recommend the subject matter areas or skills to be tested; only those knowledges or skills important to your success on the job are included. The most reliable books and source materials available are used as references. Together, the experts and technicians judge the difficulty level of the questions.

Test technicians know how to phrase questions so that the problem is clearly stated. Their ethics do not permit "trick" or "catch" questions. Questions may have been tried out on sample groups, or subjected to statistical analysis, to determine their usefulness.

Written tests are often used in combination with performance tests, ratings of training and experience, and oral interviews. All of these measures combine to form the best-known means of finding the right person for the right job.

II. HOW TO PASS THE WRITTEN TEST

A. NATURE OF THE EXAMINATION

To prepare intelligently for civil service examinations, you should know how they differ from school examinations you have taken. In school you were assigned certain definite pages to read or subjects to cover. The examination questions were quite detailed and usually emphasized memory. Civil service exams, on the other hand, try to discover your present ability to perform the duties of a position, plus your potentiality to learn these duties. In other words, a civil service exam attempts to predict how successful you will be. Questions cover such a broad area that they cannot be as minute and detailed as school exam questions.

In the public service similar kinds of work, or positions, are grouped together in one "class." This process is known as *position-classification.* All the positions in a class are paid according to the salary range for that class. One class title covers all of these positions, and they are all tested by the same examination.

B. FOUR BASIC STEPS

1) Study the announcement

How, then, can you know what subjects to study? Our best answer is: "Learn as much as possible about the class of positions for which you've applied." The exam will test the knowledge, skills and abilities needed to do the work.

Your most valuable source of information about the position you want is the official exam announcement. This announcement lists the training and experience qualifications. Check these standards and apply only if you come reasonably close to meeting them.

The brief description of the position in the examination announcement offers some clues to the subjects which will be tested. Think about the job itself. Review the duties in your mind. Can you perform them, or are there some in which you are rusty? Fill in the blank spots in your preparation.

Many jurisdictions preview the written test in the exam announcement by including a section called "Knowledge and Abilities Required," "Scope of the Examination," or some similar heading. Here you will find out specifically what fields will be tested.

2) Review your own background

Once you learn in general what the position is all about, and what you need to know to do the work, ask yourself which subjects you already know fairly well and which need improvement. You may wonder whether to concentrate on improving your strong areas or on building some background in your fields of weakness. When the announcement has specified "some knowledge" or "considerable knowledge," or has used adjectives like "beginning principles of..." or "advanced ... methods," you can get a clue as to the number and difficulty of questions to be asked in any given field. More questions, and hence broader coverage, would be included for those subjects which are more important in the work. Now weigh your strengths and weaknesses against the job requirements and prepare accordingly.

3) Determine the level of the position

Another way to tell how intensively you should prepare is to understand the level of the job for which you are applying. Is it the entering level? In other words, is this the position in which beginners in a field of work are hired? Or is it an intermediate or advanced level? Sometimes this is indicated by such words as "Junior" or "Senior" in the class title. Other jurisdictions use Roman numerals to designate the level – Clerk I, Clerk II, for example. The word "Supervisor" sometimes appears in the title. If the level is not indicated by the title, check the description of duties. Will you be working under very close supervision, or will you have responsibility for independent decisions in this work?

4) Choose appropriate study materials

Now that you know the subjects to be examined and the relative amount of each subject to be covered, you can choose suitable study materials. For beginning level jobs, or even advanced ones, if you have a pronounced weakness in some aspect of your training, read a modern, standard textbook in that field. Be sure it is up to date and has general coverage. Such books are normally available at your library, and the librarian will be glad to help you locate one. For entry-level positions, questions of appropriate difficulty are chosen – neither highly advanced questions, nor those too simple. Such questions require careful thought but not advanced training.

If the position for which you are applying is technical or advanced, you will read more advanced, specialized material. If you are already familiar with the basic principles of your field, elementary textbooks would waste your time. Concentrate on advanced textbooks and technical periodicals. Think through the concepts and review difficult problems in your field.

These are all general sources. You can get more ideas on your own initiative, following these leads. For example, training manuals and publications of the government agency which employs workers in your field can be useful, particularly for technical and professional positions. A letter or visit to the government department involved may result in more specific study suggestions, and certainly will provide you with a more definite idea of the exact nature of the position you are seeking.

III. KINDS OF TESTS

Tests are used for purposes other than measuring knowledge and ability to perform specified duties. For some positions, it is equally important to test ability to make adjustments to new situations or to profit from training. In others, basic mental abilities not dependent on information are essential. Questions which test these things may not appear as pertinent to the duties of the position as those which test for knowledge and information. Yet they are often highly important parts of a fair examination. For very general questions, it is almost impossible to help you direct your study efforts. What we can do is to point out some of the more common of these general abilities needed in public service positions and describe some typical questions.

1) General information

Broad, general information has been found useful for predicting job success in some kinds of work. This is tested in a variety of ways, from vocabulary lists to questions about current events. Basic background in some field of work, such as sociology or economics, may be sampled in a group of questions. Often these are principles which have become familiar to most persons through exposure rather than through formal training. It is difficult to advise you how to study for these questions; being alert to the world around you is our best suggestion.

2) Verbal ability

An example of an ability needed in many positions is verbal or language ability. Verbal ability is, in brief, the ability to use and understand words. Vocabulary and grammar tests are typical measures of this ability. Reading comprehension or paragraph interpretation questions are common in many kinds of civil service tests. You are given a paragraph of written material and asked to find its central meaning.

3) Numerical ability

Number skills can be tested by the familiar arithmetic problem, by checking paired lists of numbers to see which are alike and which are different, or by interpreting charts and graphs. In the latter test, a graph may be printed in the test booklet which you are asked to use as the basis for answering questions.

4) Observation

A popular test for law-enforcement positions is the observation test. A picture is shown to you for several minutes, then taken away. Questions about the picture test your ability to observe both details and larger elements.

5) Following directions

In many positions in the public service, the employee must be able to carry out written instructions dependably and accurately. You may be given a chart with several columns, each column listing a variety of information. The questions require you to carry out directions involving the information given in the chart.

6) Skills and aptitudes

Performance tests effectively measure some manual skills and aptitudes. When the skill is one in which you are trained, such as typing or shorthand, you can practice. These tests are often very much like those given in business school or high school courses. For many of the other skills and aptitudes, however, no short-time preparation can be made. Skills and abilities natural to you or that you have developed throughout your lifetime are being tested.

Many of the general questions just described provide all the data needed to answer the questions and ask you to use your reasoning ability to find the answers. Your best preparation for these tests, as well as for tests of facts and ideas, is to be at your physical and mental best. You, no doubt, have your own methods of getting into an exam-taking mood and keeping "in shape." The next section lists some ideas on this subject.

IV. KINDS OF QUESTIONS

Only rarely is the "essay" question, which you answer in narrative form, used in civil service tests. Civil service tests are usually of the short-answer type. Full instructions for answering these questions will be given to you at the examination. But in case this is your first experience with short-answer questions and separate answer sheets, here is what you need to know:

1) Multiple-choice Questions

Most popular of the short-answer questions is the "multiple choice" or "best answer" question. It can be used, for example, to test for factual knowledge, ability to solve problems or judgment in meeting situations found at work.

A multiple-choice question is normally one of three types—

- It can begin with an incomplete statement followed by several possible endings. You are to find the one ending which *best* completes the statement, although some of the others may not be entirely wrong.
- It can also be a complete statement in the form of a question which is answered by choosing one of the statements listed.
- It can be in the form of a problem – again you select the best answer.

Here is an example of a multiple-choice question with a discussion which should give you some clues as to the method for choosing the right answer:

When an employee has a complaint about his assignment, the action which will *best* help him overcome his difficulty is to

A. discuss his difficulty with his coworkers
B. take the problem to the head of the organization
C. take the problem to the person who gave him the assignment
D. say nothing to anyone about his complaint

In answering this question, you should study each of the choices to find which is best. Consider choice "A" – Certainly an employee may discuss his complaint with fellow employees, but no change or improvement can result, and the complaint remains unresolved. Choice "B" is a poor choice since the head of the organization probably does not know what assignment you have been given, and taking your problem to him is known as "going over the head" of the supervisor. The supervisor, or person who made the assignment, is the person who can clarify it or correct any injustice. Choice "C" is, therefore, correct. To say nothing, as in choice "D," is unwise. Supervisors have and interest in knowing the problems employees are facing, and the employee is seeking a solution to his problem.

2) True/False Questions

The "true/false" or "right/wrong" form of question is sometimes used. Here a complete statement is given. Your job is to decide whether the statement is right or wrong.

SAMPLE: A roaming cell-phone call to a nearby city costs less than a non-roaming call to a distant city.

This statement is wrong, or false, since roaming calls are more expensive.

This is not a complete list of all possible question forms, although most of the others are variations of these common types. You will always get complete directions for answering questions. Be sure you understand *how* to mark your answers – ask questions until you do.

V. RECORDING YOUR ANSWERS

Computer terminals are used more and more today for many different kinds of exams.

For an examination with very few applicants, you may be told to record your answers in the test booklet itself. Separate answer sheets are much more common. If this separate answer sheet is to be scored by machine – and this is often the case – it is highly important that you mark your answers correctly in order to get credit.

An electronic scoring machine is often used in civil service offices because of the speed with which papers can be scored. Machine-scored answer sheets must be marked with a pencil, which will be given to you. This pencil has a high graphite content which responds to the electronic scoring machine. As a matter of fact, stray dots may register as answers, so do not let your pencil rest on the answer sheet while you are pondering the correct answer. Also, if your pencil lead breaks or is otherwise defective, ask for another.

Since the answer sheet will be dropped in a slot in the scoring machine, be careful not to bend the corners or get the paper crumpled.

The answer sheet normally has five vertical columns of numbers, with 30 numbers to a column. These numbers correspond to the question numbers in your test booklet. After each number, going across the page are four or five pairs of dotted lines. These short dotted lines have small letters or numbers above them. The first two pairs may also have a "T" or "F" above the letters. This indicates that the first two pairs only are to be used if the questions are of the true-false type. If the questions are multiple choice, disregard the "T" and "F" and pay attention only to the small letters or numbers.

Answer your questions in the manner of the sample that follows:

32. The largest city in the United States is
    A. Washington, D.C.
    B. New York City
    C. Chicago
    D. Detroit
    E. San Francisco

1) Choose the answer you think is best. (New York City is the largest, so "B" is correct.)
2) Find the row of dotted lines numbered the same as the question you are answering. (Find row number 32)
3) Find the pair of dotted lines corresponding to the answer. (Find the pair of lines under the mark "B.")
4) Make a solid black mark between the dotted lines.

VI. BEFORE THE TEST

Common sense will help you find procedures to follow to get ready for an examination. Too many of us, however, overlook these sensible measures. Indeed, nervousness and fatigue have been found to be the most serious reasons why applicants fail to do their best on civil service tests. Here is a list of reminders:

- Begin your preparation early – Don't wait until the last minute to go scurrying around for books and materials or to find out what the position is all about.
- Prepare continuously – An hour a night for a week is better than an all-night cram session. This has been definitely established. What is more, a night a week for a month will return better dividends than crowding your study into a shorter period of time.
- Locate the place of the exam – You have been sent a notice telling you when and where to report for the examination. If the location is in a different town or otherwise unfamiliar to you, it would be well to inquire the best route and learn something about the building.
- Relax the night before the test – Allow your mind to rest. Do not study at all that night. Plan some mild recreation or diversion; then go to bed early and get a good night's sleep.
- Get up early enough to make a leisurely trip to the place for the test – This way unforeseen events, traffic snarls, unfamiliar buildings, etc. will not upset you.
- Dress comfortably – A written test is not a fashion show. You will be known by number and not by name, so wear something comfortable.
- Leave excess paraphernalia at home – Shopping bags and odd bundles will get in your way. You need bring only the items mentioned in the official notice you received; usually everything you need is provided. Do not bring reference books to the exam. They will only confuse those last minutes and be taken away from you when in the test room.
- Arrive somewhat ahead of time – If because of transportation schedules you must get there very early, bring a newspaper or magazine to take your mind off yourself while waiting.
- Locate the examination room – When you have found the proper room, you will be directed to the seat or part of the room where you will sit. Sometimes you are given a sheet of instructions to read while you are waiting. Do not fill out any forms until you are told to do so; just read them and be prepared.
- Relax and prepare to listen to the instructions
- If you have any physical problem that may keep you from doing your best, be sure to tell the test administrator. If you are sick or in poor health, you really cannot do your best on the exam. You can come back and take the test some other time.

VII. AT THE TEST

The day of the test is here and you have the test booklet in your hand. The temptation to get going is very strong. Caution! There is more to success than knowing the right answers. You must know how to identify your papers and understand variations in the type of short-answer question used in this particular examination. Follow these suggestions for maximum results from your efforts:

1) Cooperate with the monitor

The test administrator has a duty to create a situation in which you can be as much at ease as possible. He will give instructions, tell you when to begin, check to see that you are marking your answer sheet correctly, and so on. He is not there to guard you, although he will see that your competitors do not take unfair advantage. He wants to help you do your best.

2) Listen to all instructions

Don't jump the gun! Wait until you understand all directions. In most civil service tests you get more time than you need to answer the questions. So don't be in a hurry. Read each word of instructions until you clearly understand the meaning. Study the examples, listen to all announcements and follow directions. Ask questions if you do not understand what to do.

3) Identify your papers

Civil service exams are usually identified by number only. You will be assigned a number; you must not put your name on your test papers. Be sure to copy your number correctly. Since more than one exam may be given, copy your exact examination title.

4) Plan your time

Unless you are told that a test is a "speed" or "rate of work" test, speed itself is usually not important. Time enough to answer all the questions will be provided, but this does not mean that you have all day. An overall time limit has been set. Divide the total time (in minutes) by the number of questions to determine the approximate time you have for each question.

5) Do not linger over difficult questions

If you come across a difficult question, mark it with a paper clip (useful to have along) and come back to it when you have been through the booklet. One caution if you do this – be sure to skip a number on your answer sheet as well. Check often to be sure that you have not lost your place and that you are marking in the row numbered the same as the question you are answering.

6) Read the questions

Be sure you know what the question asks! Many capable people are unsuccessful because they failed to *read* the questions correctly.

7) Answer all questions

Unless you have been instructed that a penalty will be deducted for incorrect answers, it is better to guess than to omit a question.

8) Speed tests

It is often better NOT to guess on speed tests. It has been found that on timed tests people are tempted to spend the last few seconds before time is called in marking answers at random – without even reading them – in the hope of picking up a few extra points. To discourage this practice, the instructions may warn you that your score will be "corrected" for guessing. That is, a penalty will be applied. The incorrect answers will be deducted from the correct ones, or some other penalty formula will be used.

9) Review your answers

If you finish before time is called, go back to the questions you guessed or omitted to give them further thought. Review other answers if you have time.

10) Return your test materials

If you are ready to leave before others have finished or time is called, take ALL your materials to the monitor and leave quietly. Never take any test material with you. The monitor can discover whose papers are not complete, and taking a test booklet may be grounds for disqualification.

VIII. EXAMINATION TECHNIQUES

1) Read the general instructions carefully. These are usually printed on the first page of the exam booklet. As a rule, these instructions refer to the timing of the examination; the fact that you should not start work until the signal and must stop work at a signal, etc. If there are any *special* instructions, such as a choice of questions to be answered, make sure that you note this instruction carefully.

2) When you are ready to start work on the examination, that is as soon as the signal has been given, read the instructions to each question booklet, underline any key words or phrases, such as *least*, *best*, *outline*, *describe* and the like. In this way you will tend to answer as requested rather than discover on reviewing your paper that you *listed without describing*, that you selected the *worst* choice rather than the *best* choice, etc.

3) If the examination is of the objective or multiple-choice type – that is, each question will also give a series of possible answers: A, B, C or D, and you are called upon to select the best answer and write the letter next to that answer on your answer paper – it is advisable to start answering each question in turn. There may be anywhere from 50 to 100 such questions in the three or four hours allotted and you can see how much time would be taken if you read through all the questions before beginning to answer any. Furthermore, if you come across a question or group of questions which you know would be difficult to answer, it would undoubtedly affect your handling of all the other questions.

4) If the examination is of the essay type and contains but a few questions, it is a moot point as to whether you should read all the questions before starting to answer any one. Of course, if you are given a choice – say five out of seven and the like – then it is essential to read all the questions so you can eliminate the two that are most difficult. If, however, you are asked to answer all the questions, there may be danger in trying to answer the easiest one first because you may find that you will spend too much time on it. The best technique is to answer the first question, then proceed to the second, etc.

5) Time your answers. Before the exam begins, write down the time it started, then add the time allowed for the examination and write down the time it must be completed, then divide the time available somewhat as follows:

- If 3-1/2 hours are allowed, that would be 210 minutes. If you have 80 objective-type questions, that would be an average of 2-1/2 minutes per question. Allow yourself no more than 2 minutes per question, or a total of 160 minutes, which will permit about 50 minutes to review.
- If for the time allotment of 210 minutes there are 7 essay questions to answer, that would average about 30 minutes a question. Give yourself only 25 minutes per question so that you have about 35 minutes to review.

6) The most important instruction is to *read each question* and make sure you know what is wanted. The second most important instruction is to *time yourself properly* so that you answer every question. The third most important instruction is to *answer every question.* Guess if you have to but include something for each question. Remember that you will receive no credit for a blank and will probably receive some credit if you write something in answer to an essay question. If you guess a letter – say "B" for a multiple-choice question – you may have guessed right. If you leave a blank as an answer to a multiple-choice question, the examiners may respect your feelings but it will not add a point to your score. Some exams may penalize you for wrong answers, so in such cases *only,* you may not want to guess unless you have some basis for your answer.

7) Suggestions
   a. Objective-type questions
      1. Examine the question booklet for proper sequence of pages and questions
      2. Read all instructions carefully
      3. Skip any question which seems too difficult; return to it after all other questions have been answered
      4. Apportion your time properly; do not spend too much time on any single question or group of questions
      5. Note and underline key words – *all, most, fewest, least, best, worst, same, opposite,* etc.
      6. Pay particular attention to negatives
      7. Note unusual option, e.g., unduly long, short, complex, different or similar in content to the body of the question
      8. Observe the use of "hedging" words – *probably, may, most likely,* etc.
      9. Make sure that your answer is put next to the same number as the question
      10. Do not second-guess unless you have good reason to believe the second answer is definitely more correct
      11. Cross out original answer if you decide another answer is more accurate; do not erase until you are ready to hand your paper in
      12. Answer all questions; guess unless instructed otherwise
      13. Leave time for review

   b. Essay questions
      1. Read each question carefully
      2. Determine exactly what is wanted. Underline key words or phrases.
      3. Decide on outline or paragraph answer

4. Include many different points and elements unless asked to develop any one or two points or elements
5. Show impartiality by giving pros and cons unless directed to select one side only
6. Make and write down any assumptions you find necessary to answer the questions
7. Watch your English, grammar, punctuation and choice of words
8. Time your answers; don't crowd material

8) Answering the essay question

Most essay questions can be answered by framing the specific response around several key words or ideas. Here are a few such key words or ideas:

M's: manpower, materials, methods, money, management
P's: purpose, program, policy, plan, procedure, practice, problems, pitfalls, personnel, public relations

a. Six basic steps in handling problems:
   1. Preliminary plan and background development
   2. Collect information, data and facts
   3. Analyze and interpret information, data and facts
   4. Analyze and develop solutions as well as make recommendations
   5. Prepare report and sell recommendations
   6. Install recommendations and follow up effectiveness

b. Pitfalls to avoid
   1. *Taking things for granted* – A statement of the situation does not necessarily imply that each of the elements is necessarily true; for example, a complaint may be invalid and biased so that all that can be taken for granted is that a complaint has been registered
   2. *Considering only one side of a situation* – Wherever possible, indicate several alternatives and then point out the reasons you selected the best one
   3. *Failing to indicate follow up* – Whenever your answer indicates action on your part, make certain that you will take proper follow-up action to see how successful your recommendations, procedures or actions turn out to be
   4. *Taking too long in answering any single question* – Remember to time your answers properly

IX. AFTER THE TEST

Scoring procedures differ in detail among civil service jurisdictions although the general principles are the same. Whether the papers are hand-scored or graded by machine we have described, they are nearly always graded by number. That is, the person who marks the paper knows only the number – never the name – of the applicant. Not until all the papers have been graded will they be matched with names. If other tests, such as training and experience or oral interview ratings have been given, scores will be combined. Different parts of the examination usually have different weights. For example, the written test might count 60 percent of the final grade, and a rating of training and experience 40 percent. In many jurisdictions, veterans will have a certain number of points added to their grades.

After the final grade has been determined, the names are placed in grade order and an eligible list is established. There are various methods for resolving ties between those who get the same final grade – probably the most common is to place first the name of the person whose application was received first. Job offers are made from the eligible list in the order the names appear on it. You will be notified of your grade and your rank as soon as all these computations have been made. This will be done as rapidly as possible.

People who are found to meet the requirements in the announcement are called "eligibles." Their names are put on a list of eligible candidates. An eligible's chances of getting a job depend on how high he stands on this list and how fast agencies are filling jobs from the list.

When a job is to be filled from a list of eligibles, the agency asks for the names of people on the list of eligibles for that job. When the civil service commission receives this request, it sends to the agency the names of the three people highest on this list. Or, if the job to be filled has specialized requirements, the office sends the agency the names of the top three persons who meet these requirements from the general list.

The appointing officer makes a choice from among the three people whose names were sent to him. If the selected person accepts the appointment, the names of the others are put back on the list to be considered for future openings.

That is the rule in hiring from all kinds of eligible lists, whether they are for typist, carpenter, chemist, or something else. For every vacancy, the appointing officer has his choice of any one of the top three eligibles on the list. This explains why the person whose name is on top of the list sometimes does not get an appointment when some of the persons lower on the list do. If the appointing officer chooses the second or third eligible, the No. 1 eligible does not get a job at once, but stays on the list until he is appointed or the list is terminated.

X. HOW TO PASS THE INTERVIEW TEST

The examination for which you applied requires an oral interview test. You have already taken the written test and you are now being called for the interview test – the final part of the formal examination.

You may think that it is not possible to prepare for an interview test and that there are no procedures to follow during an interview. Our purpose is to point out some things you can do in advance that will help you and some good rules to follow and pitfalls to avoid while you are being interviewed.

What is an interview supposed to test?

The written examination is designed to test the technical knowledge and competence of the candidate; the oral is designed to evaluate intangible qualities, not readily measured otherwise, and to establish a list showing the relative fitness of each candidate – as measured against his competitors – for the position sought. Scoring is not on the basis of "right" and "wrong," but on a sliding scale of values ranging from "not passable" to "outstanding." As a matter of fact, it is possible to achieve a relatively low score without a single "incorrect" answer because of evident weakness in the qualities being measured.

Occasionally, an examination may consist entirely of an oral test – either an individual or a group oral. In such cases, information is sought concerning the technical knowledges and abilities of the candidate, since there has been no written examination for this purpose. More commonly, however, an oral test is used to supplement a written examination.

Who conducts interviews?

The composition of oral boards varies among different jurisdictions. In nearly all, a representative of the personnel department serves as chairman. One of the members of the board may be a representative of the department in which the candidate would work. In some cases, "outside experts" are used, and, frequently, a businessman or some other representative of the general public is asked to serve. Labor and management or other special groups may be represented. The aim is to secure the services of experts in the appropriate field.

However the board is composed, it is a good idea (and not at all improper or unethical) to ascertain in advance of the interview who the members are and what groups they represent. When you are introduced to them, you will have some idea of their backgrounds and interests, and at least you will not stutter and stammer over their names.

What should be done before the interview?

While knowledge about the board members is useful and takes some of the surprise element out of the interview, there is other preparation which is more substantive. It *is* possible to prepare for an oral interview – in several ways:

1) Keep a copy of your application and review it carefully before the interview

This may be the only document before the oral board, and the starting point of the interview. Know what education and experience you have listed there, and the sequence and dates of all of it. Sometimes the board will ask you to review the highlights of your experience for them; you should not have to hem and haw doing it.

2) Study the class specification and the examination announcement

Usually, the oral board has one or both of these to guide them. The qualities, characteristics or knowledges required by the position sought are stated in these documents. They offer valuable clues as to the nature of the oral interview. For example, if the job involves supervisory responsibilities, the announcement will usually indicate that knowledge of modern supervisory methods and the qualifications of the candidate as a supervisor will be tested. If so, you can expect such questions, frequently in the form of a hypothetical situation which you are expected to solve. NEVER go into an oral without knowledge of the duties and responsibilities of the job you seek.

3) Think through each qualification required

Try to visualize the kind of questions you would ask if you were a board member. How well could you answer them? Try especially to appraise your own knowledge and background in each area, *measured against the job sought*, and identify any areas in which you are weak. Be critical and realistic – do not flatter yourself.

4) Do some general reading in areas in which you feel you may be weak

For example, if the job involves supervision and your past experience has NOT, some general reading in supervisory methods and practices, particularly in the field of human relations, might be useful. Do NOT study agency procedures or detailed manuals. The oral board will be testing your understanding and capacity, not your memory.

5) Get a good night's sleep and watch your general health and mental attitude

You will want a clear head at the interview. Take care of a cold or any other minor ailment, and of course, no hangovers.

What should be done on the day of the interview?

Now comes the day of the interview itself. Give yourself plenty of time to get there. Plan to arrive somewhat ahead of the scheduled time, particularly if your appointment is in the fore part of the day. If a previous candidate fails to appear, the board might be ready for you a bit early. By early afternoon an oral board is almost invariably behind schedule if there are many candidates, and you may have to wait. Take along a book or magazine to read, or your application to review, but leave any extraneous material in the waiting room when you go in for your interview. In any event, relax and compose yourself.

The matter of dress is important. The board is forming impressions about you – from your experience, your manners, your attitude, and your appearance. Give your personal appearance careful attention. Dress your best, but not your flashiest. Choose conservative, appropriate clothing, and be sure it is immaculate. This is a business interview, and your appearance should indicate that you regard it as such. Besides, being well groomed and properly dressed will help boost your confidence.

Sooner or later, someone will call your name and escort you into the interview room. *This is it.* From here on you are on your own. It is too late for any more preparation. But remember, you asked for this opportunity to prove your fitness, and you are here because your request was granted.

What happens when you go in?

The usual sequence of events will be as follows: The clerk (who is often the board stenographer) will introduce you to the chairman of the oral board, who will introduce you to the other members of the board. Acknowledge the introductions before you sit down. Do not be surprised if you find a microphone facing you or a stenotypist sitting by. Oral interviews are usually recorded in the event of an appeal or other review.

Usually the chairman of the board will open the interview by reviewing the highlights of your education and work experience from your application – primarily for the benefit of the other members of the board, as well as to get the material into the record. Do not interrupt or comment unless there is an error or significant misinterpretation; if that is the case, do not hesitate. But do not quibble about insignificant matters. Also, he will usually ask you some question about your education, experience or your present job – partly to get you to start talking and to establish the interviewing "rapport." He may start the actual questioning, or turn it over to one of the other members. Frequently, each member undertakes the questioning on a particular area, one in which he is perhaps most competent, so you can expect each member to participate in the examination. Because time is limited, you may also expect some rather abrupt switches in the direction the questioning takes, so do not be upset by it. Normally, a board member will not pursue a single line of questioning unless he discovers a particular strength or weakness.

After each member has participated, the chairman will usually ask whether any member has any further questions, then will ask you if you have anything you wish to add. Unless you are expecting this question, it may floor you. Worse, it may start you off on an extended, extemporaneous speech. The board is not usually seeking more information. The question is principally to offer you a last opportunity to present further qualifications or to indicate that you have nothing to add. So, if you feel that a significant qualification or characteristic has been overlooked, it is proper to point it out in a sentence or so. Do not compliment the board on the thoroughness of their examination – they have been sketchy, and you know it. If you wish, merely say, "No thank you, I have nothing further to add." This is a point where you can "talk yourself out" of a good impression or fail to present an important bit of information. Remember, *you close the interview yourself.*

The chairman will then say, "That is all, Mr. _______, thank you." Do not be startled; the interview is over, and quicker than you think. Thank him, gather your belongings and take your leave. Save your sigh of relief for the other side of the door.

How to put your best foot forward

Throughout this entire process, you may feel that the board individually and collectively is trying to pierce your defenses, seek out your hidden weaknesses and embarrass and confuse you. Actually, this is not true. They are obliged to make an appraisal of your qualifications for the job you are seeking, and they want to see you in your best light. Remember, they must interview all candidates and a non-cooperative candidate may become a failure in spite of their best efforts to bring out his qualifications. Here are 15 suggestions that will help you:

1) Be natural – Keep your attitude confident, not cocky

If you are not confident that you can do the job, do not expect the board to be. Do not apologize for your weaknesses, try to bring out your strong points. The board is interested in a positive, not negative, presentation. Cockiness will antagonize any board member and make him wonder if you are covering up a weakness by a false show of strength.

2) Get comfortable, but don't lounge or sprawl

Sit erectly but not stiffly. A careless posture may lead the board to conclude that you are careless in other things, or at least that you are not impressed by the importance of the occasion. Either conclusion is natural, even if incorrect. Do not fuss with your clothing, a pencil or an ashtray. Your hands may occasionally be useful to emphasize a point; do not let them become a point of distraction.

3) Do not wisecrack or make small talk

This is a serious situation, and your attitude should show that you consider it as such. Further, the time of the board is limited – they do not want to waste it, and neither should you.

4) Do not exaggerate your experience or abilities

In the first place, from information in the application or other interviews and sources, the board may know more about you than you think. Secondly, you probably will not get away with it. An experienced board is rather adept at spotting such a situation, so do not take the chance.

5) If you know a board member, do not make a point of it, yet do not hide it

Certainly you are not fooling him, and probably not the other members of the board. Do not try to take advantage of your acquaintanceship – it will probably do you little good.

6) Do not dominate the interview

Let the board do that. They will give you the clues – do not assume that you have to do all the talking. Realize that the board has a number of questions to ask you, and do not try to take up all the interview time by showing off your extensive knowledge of the answer to the first one.

7) Be attentive

You only have 20 minutes or so, and you should keep your attention at its sharpest throughout. When a member is addressing a problem or question to you, give him your undivided attention. Address your reply principally to him, but do not exclude the other board members.

8) Do not interrupt

A board member may be stating a problem for you to analyze. He will ask you a question when the time comes. Let him state the problem, and wait for the question.

9) Make sure you understand the question

Do not try to answer until you are sure what the question is. If it is not clear, restate it in your own words or ask the board member to clarify it for you. However, do not haggle about minor elements.

10) Reply promptly but not hastily

A common entry on oral board rating sheets is "candidate responded readily," or "candidate hesitated in replies." Respond as promptly and quickly as you can, but do not jump to a hasty, ill-considered answer.

11) Do not be peremptory in your answers

A brief answer is proper – but do not fire your answer back. That is a losing game from your point of view. The board member can probably ask questions much faster than you can answer them.

12) Do not try to create the answer you think the board member wants

He is interested in what kind of mind you have and how it works – not in playing games. Furthermore, he can usually spot this practice and will actually grade you down on it.

13) Do not switch sides in your reply merely to agree with a board member

Frequently, a member will take a contrary position merely to draw you out and to see if you are willing and able to defend your point of view. Do not start a debate, yet do not surrender a good position. If a position is worth taking, it is worth defending.

14) Do not be afraid to admit an error in judgment if you are shown to be wrong

The board knows that you are forced to reply without any opportunity for careful consideration. Your answer may be demonstrably wrong. If so, admit it and get on with the interview.

15) Do not dwell at length on your present job

The opening question may relate to your present assignment. Answer the question but do not go into an extended discussion. You are being examined for a *new* job, not your present one. As a matter of fact, try to phrase ALL your answers in terms of the job for which you are being examined.

Basis of Rating

Probably you will forget most of these "do's" and "don'ts" when you walk into the oral interview room. Even remembering them all will not ensure you a passing grade. Perhaps you did not have the qualifications in the first place. But remembering them will help you to put your best foot forward, without treading on the toes of the board members.

Rumor and popular opinion to the contrary notwithstanding, an oral board wants you to make the best appearance possible. They know you are under pressure – but they also want to see how you respond to it as a guide to what your reaction would be under the pressures of the job you seek. They will be influenced by the degree of poise you display, the personal traits you show and the manner in which you respond.

ABOUT THIS BOOK

This book contains tests divided into Examination Sections. Go through each test, answering every question in the margin. At the end of each test look at the answer key and check your answers. On the ones you got wrong, look at the right answer choice and learn. Do not fill in the answers first. Do not memorize the questions and answers, but understand the answer and principles involved. On your test, the questions will likely be different from the samples. Questions are changed and new ones added. If you understand these past questions you should have success with any changes that arise. Tests may consist of several types of questions. We have additional books on each subject should more study be advisable or necessary for you. Finally, the more you study, the better prepared you will be. This book is intended to be the last thing you study before you walk into the examination room. Prior study of relevant texts is also recommended. NLC publishes some of these in our Fundamental Series. Knowledge and good sense are important factors in passing your exam. Good luck also helps. So now study this Passbook, absorb the material contained within and take that knowledge into the examination. Then do your best to pass that exam.

EXAMINATION SECTION

EXAMINATION SECTION
TEST 1

DIRECTIONS: Each question or incomplete statement is followed by several suggested answers or completions. Select the one that *BEST* answers the question or completes the statement. *PRINT THE LETTER OF THE CORRECT ANSWER IN THE SPACE AT THE RIGHT.*

Questions 1-5.

DIRECTIONS: Each question from 1 to 5 consists of a sentence with an underlined word. For each question, select the choice that is *CLOSEST* in meaning to the underlined word.

EXAMPLE

This division reviews the fiscal reports of the agency.
In this sentence the word *fiscal* means most nearly

A. financial B. critical C. basic D. personnel

The correct answer is A. "financial" because "financial" is closest to *fiscal*. Therefore, the answer is A.

1. Every good office worker needs basic skills. 1.____
The word *basic* in this sentence means

A. fundamental B. advanced C. unusual D. outstanding

2. He turned out to be a good instructor. 2.____
The word *instructor* in this sentence means

A. student B. worker C. typist D. teacher

3. The quantity of work in the office was under study. 3.____
In this sentence, the word *quantity* means

A. amount B. flow C. supervision D. type

4. The morning was spent examining the time records. 4.____
In this sentence, the word *examining* means

A. distributing B. collecting C. checking D. filing

5. The candidate filled in the proper spaces on the form. 5.____
In this sentence, the word *proper* means

A. blank B. appropriate C. many D. remaining

Questions 6-8.

DIRECTIONS: You are to answer Questions 6 through 8 *SOLELY* on the basis of the information contained in the following paragraph:

The increase in the number of public documents in the last two centuries closely matches the increase in population in the United States. The great number of public documents has become a serious threat to their usefulness. It is necessary to have programs which will reduce the number of public documents that are kept and which will, at the same time, assure keeping those that have value. Such programs need a great deal of thought to have any success.

6. According to the above paragraph, public documents may be less useful if 6.____

   A. the files are open to the public
   B. the record room is too small
   C. the copying machine is operated only during normal working hours
   D. too many records are being kept

7. According to the above paragraph, the growth of the population in the United States has matched the growth in the quantity of public documents for a period of, most nearly, 7.____

   A. 50 years B. 100 years C. 200 years D. 300 years

8. According to the above paragraph, the increased number of public documents has made it necessary to 8.____

   A. find out which public documents are worth keeping
   B. reduce the great number of public documents by decreasing government services
   C. eliminate the copying of all original public documents
   D. avoid all new copying devices.

Questions 9-10.

DIRECTIONS: You are to answer Questions 9 and 10 *SOLELY* on the basis of the information contained in the following paragraph:

The work goals of an agency can best be reached if the employees understand and agree with these goals. One way to gain such understanding and agreement is for management to encourage and seriously consider suggestions from employees in the setting of agency goals.

9. On the basis of the paragraph above, the *BEST* way to achieve the work goals of an agency is to 9.____

   A. make certain that employees work as hard as possible
   B. study the organizational structure of the agency
   C. encourage employees to think seriously about the agency's problems
   D. stimulate employee understanding of the work goals

10. On the basis of the paragraph above, understanding and agreement with agency goals can be gained by 10.____

   A. allowing the employees to set agency goals
   B. reaching agency goals quickly
   C. legislative review of agency operations
   D. employee participation in setting agency goals

Questions 11-15.

DIRECTIONS: Each of Questions 11 through 15 consists of a group of four words. One word in each group is *INCORRECTLY* spelled. For each question, print the letter of the correct answer in the space at the right that is the same as the letter next to the word which is *INCORRECTLY* spelled.

EXAMPLE

A. housing B. certain C. budgit D. money

The word "budgit" is incorrectly spelled, because the correct spelling should be "budget." Therefore, the correct answer is C.

11.	A. sentince	B. bulletin	C. notice	D. definition	11.____
12.	A. appointment	B. exactly	C. typest	D. light	12.____
13.	A. penalty	B. suparvise	C. consider	D. division	13.____
14.	A. schedule	B. accurate	C. corect	D. simple	14.____
15.	A. suggestion	B. installed	C. proper	D. agincy	15.____

Questions 16-20.

DIRECTIONS: Each question from 16 through 20 consists of a sentence which may be
A. incorrect because of bad word usage, or
B. incorrect because of bad punctuation, or
C. incorrect because of bad spelling, or
D. correct

Read each sentence carefully. Then print in the proper space at the right A, B, C, or D, according to the answer you choose from the four choices listed above. There is only one type of error in each incorrect sentence. If there is no error, the sentence is correct.

EXAMPLE

George Washington was the father of his contry.
This sentence is incorrect because of bad spelling ("contry" instead of "country"). Therefore, the answer is C.

16. The assignment was completed in record time but the payroll for it has not yet been preparid. 16.____

17. The operator, on the other hand, is willing to learn me how to use the mimeograph. 17.____

18. She is the prettiest of the three sisters. 18.____

19. She doesn't know; if the mail has arrived. 19.____

20. The doorknob of the office door is broke. 20.____

21. A clerk can process a form in 15 minutes. How many forms can that clerk process in six hours? 21.____

    A. 10 B. 21 C. 24 D. 90

22. An office staff consists of 120 people. Sixty of them have been assigned to a special project. Of the remaining staff, 20 answer the mail, 10-handle phone calls, and the rest operate the office machines. The number of people operating the office machines is 22.____

    A. 20 B. 30 C. 40 D. 45

23. An office worker received 65 applications but on the first day had to return 26 of them for being incomplete and on the second day 25 had to be returned for being incomplete. How many applications did <u>not</u> have to be returned? 23.____

    A. 10 B. 12 C. 14 D. 16

24. An office worker answered 63 phone calls in one day and 91 phone calls the next day. For these 2 days, what was the average number of phone calls he answered per day? 24.____

A. 77 B. 28 C. 82 D. 93

25. An office worker processed 12 vouchers of $8.75 each, 3 vouchers of $3.68 each, and 2 vouchers of $1.29 each. The total dollar amount of these vouchers is 25.____

A. $116.04 B. $117.52 C. $118.62 D. $119.04

KEY (CORRECT ANSWERS)

1. A
2. D
3. A
4. C
5. B
6. D
7. C
8. A
9. D
10. D
11. A
12. C
13. B
14. C
15. D
16. C
17. A
18. D
19. B
20. A
21. C
22. B
23. C
24. A
25. C

TEST 2

DIRECTIONS: Each question or incomplete statement is followed by several suggested answers or completions. Select the one that *BEST* answers the question or completes the statement. *PRINT THE LETTER OF THE CORRECT ANSWER IN THE SPACE AT THE RIGHT.*

Questions 1-5.

DIRECTIONS: Each question from 1 to 5 lists four names. The names may or may not be exactly the same. Compare the names in each question and mark your answer as follows:

Mark your answer A if all the names are different
Mark your answer B if only two names are exactly the same
Mark your answer C if only three names are exactly the same
Mark your answer D if all four names are exactly the same

EXAMPLE

Jensen, Alfred E.
Jensen, Alfred E.
Jensan, Alfred E.
Jensen, Fred E.

Since the name Jensen, Alfred E. appears twice and is exactly the same in both places, the correct answer is B.

1. Riviera, Pedro S. 1.____
   Rivers, Pedro S.
   Riviera, Pedro N.
   Riviera, Juan S.

2. Guider, Albert 2.____
   Guidar, Albert
   Giuder, Alfred
   Guider, Albert

3. Blum, Rona 3.____
   Blum, Rona
   Blum, Rona
   Blum, Rona

4. Raugh, John 4.____
   Raugh, James
   Raughe, John
   Raugh, John

5. Katz, Stanley 5.____
   Katz, Stanley
   Katze, Stanley
   Katz, Stanley

Questions 6-10.

DIRECTIONS: Each Question 6 through 10 consists of numbers or letters in Columns I and II. For each question, compare each line of Column I with its corresponding line in Column II and decide how many lines in Column I are *EXACTLY* the same as their corresponding lines in Column II. In your answer space, mark your answer as follows:

Mark your answer A if only *ONE* line in Column I is exactly the same as its corresponding line in Column II
Mark your answer B if only *TWO* lines in Column I are exactly the same as their corresponding lines in Column II
Mark your answer C if only *THREE* lines in Column I are exactly the same as their corresponding lines in Column II
Mark your answer D if all *FOUR* lines in Column I are exactly the same as their corresponding lines in Column II

EXAMPLE

Column I	Column II
1776	1776
1865	1865
1945	1945
1976	1978

Only three lines in Column I are exactly the same as their corresponding lines in Column II. Therefore, the correct answer is C.

	Column I	Column II	
6.	5653	5653	6.____
	8727	8728	
	ZPSS	ZPSS	
	4952	9453	
7.	PNJP	PNPJ	7.____
	NJPJ	NJPJ	
	JNPN	JNPN	
	PNJP	PNPJ	
8.	effe	eFfe	8.____
	uWvw	uWvw	
	KpGj	KpGg	
	vmnv	vmnv	
9.	5232	5232	9.____
	PfrC	PfrN	
	zssz	zzss	
	rwwr	rwww	
10.	czws	czws	10.____
	cecc	cece	
	thrm	thrm	
	lwtz	lwtz	

Questions 11-15.

DIRECTIONS: Questions 11 through 15 have lines of letters and numbers. Each letter should be matched with its number in accordance with the following table:

Letter	F	R	C	A	W	L	E	N	B	T
Matching Number	0	1	2	3	4	5	6	7	8	9

From the table you can determine that the letter F has the matching number 0 below it, the letter R has the matching number 1 below it, etc.

For each question, compare each line of letters and numbers carefully to see if each letter has its correct matching number. If all the letters and numbers are matched correctly in

none of the lines of the question, mark your answer A
only *one* of the lines of the question, mark your answer B
only *two* of the lines of the question, mark your answer C
all three lines of the question, mark your answer D

EXAMPLE

WBCR 4826
TLBF 9580
ATNE 3986

There is a mistake in the first line because the letter R should have its matching number 1 instead of the number 6.

The second line is correct because each letter shown has the correct matching number.

There is a mistake in the third line because the letter N should have the matching number 7 instead of the number 8,

Since all the letters and numbers are matched correctly in only one of the lines in the sample, the correct answer is B.

11. EBCT 6829 11.____
ATWR 3961
NLBW 7584

12. RNCT 1729 12.____
LNCR 5728
WAEB 5368

13. NTWB 7948 13.____
RABL 1385
TAEF 9360

14. LWRB 5417 14.____
RLWN 1647
CBWA 2843

15. ABTC 3792 15.____
WCER 5261
AWCN 3417

16. Your job often brings you into contact with the public. Of the following, it would be *MOST* desirable to explain the reasons for official actions to people coming into your office for assistance because such explanations 16.____

A. help build greater understanding between the public and your agency
B. help build greater self-confidence in city employees
C. convince the public that nothing they do can upset a city employee
D. show the public that city employees are intelligent

17. Assume that you strongly dislike one of your co-workers. 17.____
You should *FIRST*

A. discuss your feeling with the co-worker
B. demand a transfer to another office
C. suggest to your supervisor that the co-worker should be observed carefully
D. try to figure out the reason for this dislike before you say or do anything

18. An office worker who has problems accepting authority is *MOST* likely to find it difficult to 18.____

A. obey rules
B. understand people
C. assist other employees
D. follow complex instructions

19. The employees in your office have taken a dislike to one person and frequently annoy her. Your supervisor *should* 19.____

A. transfer this person to another unit at the first opportunity
B. try to find out the reason for the staff's attitude before doing anything about it
C. threaten to transfer the first person observed bothering this person
D. ignore the situation

20. Assume that your supervisor has asked a worker in your office to get a copy of a report out of the files. You notice the worker has accidentally pulled out the wrong report. Of the following, the *BEST* way for you to handle this situation is to tell 20.____

A. the worker about all the difficulties that will result from this error
B. the worker about her mistake in a nice way
C. the worker to ignore this error
D. your supervisor that this worker needs more training in how to use the files

21. Filing systems differ in their efficiency. Which of the following is the *BEST* way to evaluate the efficiency of a filing system? 21.____
The

A. number of times used per day
B. amount of material that is received each day for filing
C. amount of time it takes to locate material
D. type of locking system used

22. In planning ahead so that a sufficient amount of general office supplies is always available, it would be *LEAST* important to find out the 22.____

A. current office supply needs of the staff
B. amount of office supplies used last year
C. days and times that office supplies can be ordered
D. agency goals and objectives

23. The *MAIN* reason for establishing routine office work procedures is that once a routine is established 23.____

A. work need not be checked for accuracy
B. all steps in the routine will take an equal amount of time to perform
C. each time the job is repeated it will take less time to perform
D. each step in the routine will not have to be planned all over again each time

24. When an office machine centrally located in an agency must be shut down for repairs, the bureaus and divisions using this machine should be informed of the 24.____

A. expected length of time before the machine will be in operation again
B. estimated cost of repairs
C. efforts being made to avoid future repairs
D. type of new equipment which the agency may buy in the future to replace the machine being repaired

25. If the day's work is properly scheduled, the *MOST* important result would be that the 25.____

A. supervisor will not have to do much supervision
B. employee will know what to do next
C. employee will show greater initiative
D. job will become routine

KEY (CORRECT ANSWERS)

1. A
2. B
3. D
4. B
5. C

6. B
7. B
8. B
9. A
10. C

11. C
12. B
13. D
14. B
15. A

16. A
17. D
18. A
19. B
20. B

21. C
22. D
23. D
24. A
25. B

EXAMINATION SECTION
TEST 1

DIRECTIONS: Each question or incomplete statement is followed by several suggested answers or completions. Select the one that BEST answers the question or completes the statement. *PRINT THE LETTER OF THE CORRECT ANSWER IN THE SPACE AT THE RIGHT.*

1. Assume that a few co-workers meet near your desk and talk about personal matters during working hours. Lately, this practice has interfered with your work. 1.____
   In order to stop this practice, the BEST action for you to take FIRST is to

   A. ask your supervisor to put a stop to the co-workers' meeting near your desk
   B. discontinue any friendship with this group
   C. ask your co-workers not to meet near your desk
   D. request that your desk be moved to another location

2. In order to maintain office coverage during working hours, your supervisor has scheduled your lunch hour from 1 P.M. to 2 P.M. and your co-worker's lunch hour from 12 P.M. to 1 P.M. Lately, your co-worker has been returning late from lunch each day. As a result, you don't get a full hour since you must return to the office by 2 P.M. 2.____
   Of the following, the BEST action for you to take FIRST is to

   A. explain to your co-worker in a courteous manner that his lateness is interfering with your right to a full hour for lunch
   B. tell your co-worker that his lateness must stop or you will report him to your supervisor
   C. report your co-worker's lateness to your supervisor
   D. leave at 1 P.M. for lunch, whether your co-worker has returned or not

3. Assume that, as an office worker, one of your jobs is to open mail sent to your unit, read the mail for content, and send the mail to the appropriate person to handle. You accidentally open and begin to read a letter marked *personal* addressed to a co-worker. 3.____
   Of the following, the BEST action for you to take is to

   A. report to your supervisor that your co-worker is receiving personal mail at the office
   B. destroy the letter so that your co-worker does not know you saw it
   C. reseal the letter and place it on the co-worker's desk without saying anything
   D. bring the letter to your co-worker and explain that you opened it by accident

4. Suppose that in evaluating your work, your supervisor gives you an overall good rating, but states that you sometimes turn in work with careless errors. 4.____
   The BEST action for you to take would be to

   A. ask a co-worker who is good at details to proofread your work
   B. take time to do a careful job, paying more attention to detail
   C. continue working as usual since occasional errors are to be expected
   D. ask your supervisor if she would mind correcting your errors

5. Assume that you are taking a telephone message for a co-worker who is not in the office at the time. 5.____
   Of the following, the LEAST important item to write on the message is the

   A. length of the call
   B. name of the caller
   C. time of the call
   D. telephone number of the caller

Questions 6-13.

DIRECTIONS: Questions 6 through 13 each consist of a sentence which may or may not be an example of good English. The underlined parts of each sentence may be correct or incorrect. Examine each sentence, considering grammar, punctuation, spelling, and capitalization. If the English usage in the underlined parts of the sentence given is better than any of the changes in the underlined words suggested in Options B, C, or D, choose Option A. If the changes in the underlined words suggested in Options B, C, or D would make the sentence correct, choose the correct option. Do not choose an option that will change the meaning of the sentence.

6. This Fall, the office will be closed on Columbus Day, October 9th. 6.____

A. Correct as is
B. fall...Columbus Day, October
C. Fall...columbus day, October
D. fall...Columbus Day, october

7. This manual discribes the duties performed by an Office Aide. 7.____

A. Correct as is
B. describe the duties performed
C. discribe the duties performed
D. describes the duties performed

8. There weren't no paper in the supply closet. 8.____

A. Correct as is
B. weren't any
C. wasn't any
D. wasn't no

9. The new employees left there office to attend a meeting. 9.____

A. Correct as is
B. they're
C. their
D. thier

10. The office worker started working at 8;30 a.m. 10.____

A. Correct as is
B. 8:30 a.m.
C. 8;30 a,m.
D. 8:30 am.

11. The alphabet, or A to Z sequence are the basis of most filing systems. 11.____

A. Correct as is
B. alphabet, or A to Z sequence, is
C. alphabet, or A to Z sequence are
D. alphabet, or A too Z sequence, is

12. Those file cabinets are five feet tall. 12.____

A. Correct as is
B. Them...feet
C. Those...foot
D. Them...foot

13. The Office Aide checked the register and finding the date of the meeting. 13.____

A. Correct as is
B. regaster and finding
C. register and found
D. regaster and found

Questions 14-21.

DIRECTIONS: Each of Questions 14 through 21 has two lists of numbers. Each list contains three sets of numbers. Check each of the three sets in the list on the right to see if they are the same as the corresponding set in the list on the left. Mark your answers:

A. If none of the sets in the right list are the same as those in the left list
B. if only one of the sets in the right list are the same as those in the left list
C. if only two of the sets in the right list are the same as those in the left list
D. if all three sets in the right list are the same as those in the left list

14.	7354183476 4474747744 57914302311	7354983476 4474747774 57914302311	14.____
15.	7143592185 8344517699 9178531263	7143892185 8344518699 9178531263	15.____
16.	2572114731 8806835476 8255831246	257214731 8806835476 8255831246	16.____
17.	331476853821 6976658532996 3766042113715	331476858621 6976655832996 3766042113745	17.____
18.	8806663315 74477138449 211756663666	8806663315 74477138449 211756663666	18.____
19.	990006966996 53022219743 4171171117717	99000696996 53022219843 4171171177717	19.____
20.	24400222433004 5300030055000355 20000075532002022	24400222433004 5300030055500355 20000075532002022	20.____
21.	611166640660001116 7111300117001100733 26666446664476518	61116664066001116 7111300117001100733 26666446664476518	21.____

Questions 22-25.

DIRECTIONS: Each of Questions 22 through 25 has two lists of names and addresses. Each list contains three sets of names and addresses. Check each of the three sets in the list on the right to see if they are the same as the corresponding set in the list on the left. Mark your answers:

A. if none of the sets in the right list are the same as those in the left list
B. if only one of the sets in the right list is the same as those in the left list
C. if only two of the sets in the right list are the same as those in the the left list
D. if all three sets in the right list are the same as those in the left list

22.	Mary T. Berlinger 2351 Hampton St. Monsey, N.Y. 20117	Mary T. Berlinger 2351 Hampton St. Monsey, N.Y. 20117	22.____
	Eduardo Benes 473 Kingston Avenue Central Islip, N.Y. 11734	Eduardo Benes 473 Kingston Avenue Central Islip, N.Y. 11734	
	Alan Carrington Fuchs 17 Gnarled Hollow Road Los Angeles, CA 91635	Alan Carrington Fuchs 17 Gnarled Hollow Road Los Angeles, CA 91685	
23.	David John Jacobson 178 35 St. Apt. 4C New York, N.Y. 00927	David John Jacobson 178 53 St. Apt. 4C New York, N.Y. 00927	23.____
	Ann-Marie Calonella 7243 South Ridge Blvd. Bakersfield, CA 96714	Ann-Marie Calonella 7243 South Ridge Blvd. Bakersfield, CA 96714	
	Pauline M. Thompson 872 Linden Ave. Houston, Texas 70321	Pauline M. Thomson 872 Linden Ave. Houston, Texas 70321	
24.	Chester LeRoy Masterton 152 Lacy Rd. Kankakee, Ill. 54532	Chester LeRoy Masterson 152 Lacy Rd. Kankakee, Ill. 54532	24.____
	William Maloney S. LaCrosse Pla. Wausau, Wisconsin 52146	William Maloney S. LaCross Pla. Wausau, Wisconsin 52146	
	Cynthia V. Barnes 16 Pines Rd. Greenpoint, Miss. 20376	Cynthia V. Barnes 16 Pines Rd. Greenpoint, Miss. 20376	

25.	Marcel Jean Frontenac 6 Burton On The Water Calender, Me. 01471	Marcel Jean Frontenac 6 Burton On The Water Calender, Me. 01471	25.____
	J. Scott Marsden 174 S. Tipton St. Cleveland, Ohio	J. Scott Marsden 174 Tipton St. Cleveland, Ohio	
	Lawrence T. Haney 171 McDonough St. Decatur, Ga. 31304	Lawrence T. Haney 171 McDonough St. Decatur, Ga. 31304	

KEY (CORRECT ANSWERS)

1.	C	11.	B
2.	A	12.	A
3.	D	13.	C
4.	B	14.	B
5.	A	15.	B
6.	A	16.	C
7.	D	17.	A
8.	C	18.	D
9.	C	19.	A
10.	B	20.	C

21. C
22. C
23. B
24. B
25. C

TEST 2

DIRECTIONS: Each question or incomplete statement is followed by several suggested answers or completions. Select the one that BEST answers the question or completes the statement. *PRINT THE LETTER OF THE CORRECT ANSWER IN THE SPACE AT THE RIGHT.*

Questions 1-6.

DIRECTIONS: Questions 1 through 6 are to be answered SOLELY on the basis of the information contained in the following passage.

Duplicating is the process of making a number of identical copies of letters, documents, etc. from an original. Some duplicating processes make copies directly from the original document. Other duplicating processes require the preparation of a special master, and copies are then made from the master. Four of the most common duplicating processes are stencil, fluid, offset, and xerox.

In the stencil process, the typewriter is used to cut the words into a master called a stencil. Drawings, charts, or graphs can be cut into the stencil using a stylus. As many as 3,500 good-quality copies can be reproduced from one stencil. Various grades of finished paper from inexpensive mimeograph to expensive bond can be used.

The fluid process is a good method of copying from 50 to 125 good-quality copies from a master, which is prepared with a special dye. The master is placed on the duplicator, and special paper with a hard finish is moistened and then passed through the duplicator. Some of the dye on the master is dissolved, creating an impression on the paper. The impression becomes lighter as more copies are made; and once the dye on the master is used up, a new master must be made.

The offset process is the most adaptable office duplicating process because this process can be used for making a few copies or many copies. Masters can be made on paper or plastic for a few hundred copies, or on metal plates for as many as 75,000 copies. By using a special technique called photo-offset, charts, photographs, illustrations, or graphs can be reproduced on the master plate. The offset process is capable of producing large quantities of fine, top-quality copies on all types of finished paper.

The xerox process reproduces an exact duplicate from an original. It is the fastest duplicating method because the original material is placed directly on the duplicator, eliminating the need to make a special master. Any kind of paper can be used. The xerox process is the most expensive duplicating process; however, it is the best method of reproducing small quantities of good-quality copies of reports, letters, official documents, memos, or contracts.

1. Of the following, the MOST efficient method of reproducing 5,000 copies of a graph is 1.____

   A. stencil B. fluid C. offset D. xerox

2. The offset process is the MOST adaptable office duplicating process because 2.____

   A. it is the quickest duplicating method
   B. it is the least expensive duplicating method
   C. it can produce a small number or large number of copies
   D. a softer master can be used over and over again

3. Which one of the following duplicating processes uses moistened paper? 3.____

A. Stencil B. Fluid C. Offset D. Xerox

4. The fluid process would be the BEST process to use for reproducing 4.____

A. five copies of a school transcript
B. fifty copies of a memo
C. five hundred copies of a form letter
D. five thousand copies of a chart

5. Which one of the following duplicating processes does NOT require a special master? 5.____

A. Fluid B. Xerox C. Offset D. Stencil

6. Xerox is NOT used for all duplicating jobs because 6.____

A. it produces poor-quality copies
B. the process is too expensive
C. preparing the master is too time-consuming
D. it cannot produce written reports

7. Assume a city agency has 775 office workers. 7.____
If 2 out of 25 office workers were absent on a particular day, how many office workers reported to work on that day?

A. 713 B. 744 C. 750 D. 773

Questions 8-11.

DIRECTIONS: In Questions 8 through 11, select the choice that is CLOSEST in meaning to the underlined word.

SAMPLE: This division reviews the <u>fiscal</u> reports of the agency.
In this sentence, the word <u>fiscal</u> means MOST NEARLY
A. financial B. critical C. basic D. personnel

The correct answer is A, financial, because financial is closest to <u>fiscal</u>.

8. A central file eliminates the need to <u>retain</u> duplicate material. 8.____
The word <u>retain</u> means MOST NEARLY

A. keep B. change C. locate D. process

9. Filing is a <u>routine</u> office task. 9.____
<u>Routine</u> means MOST NEARLY

A. proper B. regular C. simple D. difficult

10. Sometimes a word, phrase, or sentence must be <u>deleted</u> to correct an error. 10.____
<u>Deleted</u> means MOST NEARLY

A. removed B. added C. expanded D. improved

11. Your supervisor will evaluate your work. 11.____
Evaluate means MOST NEARLY

A. judge B. list C. assign D. explain

Questions 12-19.

DIRECTIONS: The code table below shows 10 letters with matching numbers. For each Question 12 through 19, there are three sets of letters. Each set of letters is followed by a set of numbers which may or may not match their correct letter according to the code table. For each question, check all three sets of letters and numbers and mark your answer:
A. if no pairs are correctly matched
B. if only one pair is correctly matched
C. if only two pairs are correctly matched
D. if all three pairs are correctly matched

CODE TABLE

T	M	V	D	S	P	R	G	B	H
1	2	3	4	5	6	7	8	9	0

Sample Question:
TMVDSP - 123456
RGBHTM - 789011
DSPRGB - 256789

In the sample question above, the first set of numbers correctly matches its set of letters. But the second and third pairs contain mistakes. In the second pair, M is incorrectly matched with number 1. According to the code table, letter M should be correctly matched with number 2. In the third pair, the letter D is incorrectly matched with number 2. According to the code table, letter D should be correctly matched with number 4. Since only one of the pairs is correctly matched, the answer to this sample question is B.

12. RSBMRM - 759262 12.____
GDSRVH - 845730
VDBRTM - 349713

13. TGVSDR - 183247 13.____
SMHRDP - 520647
TRMHSR - 172057

14. DSPRGM - 456782 14.____
MVDBHT - 234902
HPMDBT - 062491

15. BVPTRD - 936184 15.____
GDPHMB - 807029
GMRHMV - 827032

16. MGVRSH - 283750 16.____
TRDMBS - 174295
SPRMGV - 567283

17. SGBSDM - 489542 17.____
MGHPTM - 290612
MPBMHT - 269301

18. TDPBHM - 146902 18.____
VPBMRS - 369275
GDMBHM - 842902

19. MVPTBV - 236194 19.____
PDRTMB - 647128
BGTMSM - 981232

Questions 20-25.

DIRECTIONS: In each of Questions 20 through 25, the names of four people are given. For each question, choose as your answer the one of the four names given which should be filed FIRST according to the usual system of alphabetical filing of names, as described in the following paragraph.

In filing names, you must start with the last name. Names are filed in order of the first letter of the last name, then the second letter, etc. Therefore, BAILY would be filed before BROWN, which would be filed before COLT. A name with fewer letters of the same type comes first; i.e., Smith before Smithe. If the last names are the same, the names are filed alphabetically by the first name. If the first name is an initial, a name with an initial would come before a first name that starts with the same letter as the initial. Therefore, I. BROWN would come before IRA BROWN. Finally, if both last name and first name are the same, the name would be filed alphabetically by the middle name, one again an initial coming before a middle name which starts with the same letter as the initial. If there is no middle name at all, the name would come before those with middle initials or names.

Sample Question: A. Lester Daniels
B. William Dancer
C. Nathan Danzig
D. Dan Lester

The last names beginning with D are filed before the last name beginning with L. Since DANIELS, DANCER, and DANZIG all begin with the same three letters, you must look at the fourth letter of the last name to determine which name should be filed first. C comes before I or Z in the alphabet, so DANCER is filed before DANIELS or DANZIG. Therefore, the answer to the above sample question is B.

20. A. Scott Biala B. Mary Byala 20.____
C. Martin Baylor D. Francis Bauer

21. A. Howard J. Black B. Howard Black 21.____
C. J. Howard Black D. John H. Black

22. A. Theodora Garth Kingston B. Theadore Barth Kingston 22.____
C. Thomas Kingston D. Thomas T. Kingston

23. A. Paulette Mary Huerta B. Paul M. Huerta 23.____
C. Paulette L. Huerta D. Peter A. Huerta

24. A. Martha Hunt Morgan B. Martin Hunt Morgan 24.____
C. Mary H. Morgan D. Martine H. Morgan

25. A. James T. Meerschaum B. James M. Mershum 25.____
C. James F. Mearshaum D. James N. Meshum

KEY (CORRECT ANSWERS)

1.	C	11.	A
2.	C	12.	B
3.	B	13.	B
4.	B	14.	C
5.	B	15.	A
6.	B	16.	D
7.	A	17.	A
8.	A	18.	D
9.	B	19.	A
10.	A	20.	D

21. B
22. B
23. B
24. A
25. C

TEST 3

DIRECTIONS: Each question or incomplete statement is followed by several suggested answers or completions. Select the one that BEST answers the question or completes the statement. *PRINT THE LETTER OF THE CORRECT ANSWER IN THE SPACE AT THE RIGHT.*

1. Which one of the following statements about proper telephone usage is NOT always correct? 1.____
When answering the telephone, you should

   A. know whom you are speaking to
   B. give the caller your undivided attention
   C. identify yourself to the caller
   D. obtain the information the caller wishes before you do your other work

2. Assume that, as a member of a worker's safety committee in your agency, you are responsible for encouraging other employees to follow correct safety practices. While you are working on your regular assignment, you observe an employee violating a safety rule. 2.____
Of the following, the BEST action for you to take FIRST is to

   A. speak to the employee about safety practices and order him to stop violating the safety rule
   B. speak to the employee about safety practices and point out the safety rule he is violating
   C. bring the matter up in the next committee meeting
   D. report this violation of the safety rule to the employee's supervisor

3. Assume that you have been temporarily assigned by your supervisor to do a job which you do not want to do. The BEST action for you to take is to 3.____

   A. discuss the job with your supervisor, explaining why you do not want to do it
   B. discuss the job with your supervisor and tell her that you will not do it
   C. ask a co-worker to take your place on this job
   D. do some other job that you like; your supervisor may give the job you do not like to someone else

4. Assume that you keep the confidential personnel files of employees in your unit. A friend asks you to obtain some information from the file of one of your co-workers. 4.____
The BEST action to take is to ______ to your friend.

   A. ask the co-worker if you can give the information
   B. ask your supervisor if you can give the information
   C. give the information
   D. refuse to give the information

Questions 5-8.

DIRECTIONS: Questions 5 through 8 are to be answered SOLELY on the basis of the information contained in the following passage.

City government is committed to providing a safe and healthy work environment for all city employees. An effective agency safety program reduces accidents by educating employees about the types of careless acts which can cause accidents. Even in an office, accidents can happen. If each employee is aware of possible safety hazards, the number of accidents on the job can be reduced.

Careless use of office equipment can cause accidents and injuries. For example, file cabinet drawers which are filled with papers can be so heavy that the entire cabinet could tip over from the weight of one open drawer.

The bottom drawers of desks and file cabinets should never be left open since employees could easily trip over open drawers and injure themselves.

When reaching for objects on a high shelf, an employee should use a strong, sturdy object such as a step stool to stand on. Makeshift platforms made out of books, papers, or boxes can easily collapse. Even chairs can slide out from under foot, causing serious injury.

Even at an employee's desk, safety hazards can occur. Frayed or cut wires should be repaired or replaced immediately. Computers which are not firmly anchored to the desk or table could fall, causing injury.

Smoking is one of the major causes of fires in the office. A lighted match or improperly extinguished cigarette thrown into a wastebasket filled with paper could cause a major fire with possible loss of life. Where smoking is permitted, ashtrays should be used. Smoking is particularly dangerous in offices where flammable chemicals are used.

5. The goal of an effective safety program is to 5.____

   A. reduce office accidents
   B. stop employees from smoking on the job
   C. encourage employees to continue their education
   D. eliminate high shelves in offices

6. Desks and file cabinets can become safety hazards when 6.____

   A. their drawers are left open
   B. they are used as wastebaskets
   C. they are makeshift
   D. they are not anchored securely to the floor

7. Smoking is especially hazardous when it occurs 7.____

   A. near exposed wires
   B. in a crowded office
   C. in an area where flammable chemicals are used
   D. where books and papers are stored

8. Accidents are likely to occur when 8.____

   A. employees' desks are cluttered with books and papers
   B. employees are not aware of safety hazards
   C. employees close desk drawers
   D. step stools are used to reach high objects

9. Assume that part of your job as a worker in the accounting division of a city agency is to answer the telephone. When you first answer the telephone, it is LEAST important to tell the caller 9.____

A. your title
B. your name
C. the name of your unit
D. the name of your agency

10. Assume that you are assigned to work as a receptionist, and your duties are to answer phones, greet visitors, and do other general office work. You are busy with a routine job when several visitors approach your desk. 10.____
The BEST action to take is to

A. ask the visitors to have a seat and assist them after your work is completed
B. tell the visitors that you are busy and they should return at a more convenient time
C. stop working long enough to assist the visitors
D. continue working and wait for the visitors to ask you for assistance

11. Assume that your supervisor has chosen you to take a special course during working hours to learn a new payroll procedure. Although you know that you were chosen because of your good work record, a co-worker, who feels that he should have been chosen, has been telling everyone in your unit that the choice was unfair. 11.____
Of the following, the BEST way to handle this situation FIRST is to

A. suggest to the co-worker that everything in life is unfair
B. contact your union representative in case your co-worker presents a formal grievance
C. tell your supervisor about your co-worker's complaints and let her handle the situation
D. tell the co-worker that you were chosen because of your superior work record

12. Assume that while you are working on an assignment which must be completed quickly, a supervisor from another unit asks you to obtain information for her. 12.____
Of the following, the BEST way to respond to her request is to

A. tell her to return in an hour since you are busy
B. give her the names of some people in her own unit who could help her
C. tell her you are busy and refer her to a co-worker
D. tell her that you are busy and ask her if she could wait until you finish your assignment

13. A co-worker in your unit is often off from work because of illness. Your supervisor assigns the co-worker's work to you when she is not there. Lately, doing her work has interfered with your own job. 13.____
The BEST action for you to take FIRST is to

A. discuss the problem with your supervisor
B. complete your own work before starting your co-worker's work
C. ask other workers in your unit to assist you
D. work late in order to get the jobs done

14. During the month of June, 40,587 people attended a city-owned swimming pool. In July, 13,014 more people attended the swimming pool than the number that had attended in June. In August, 39,655 people attended the swimming pool. 14.____
The TOTAL number of people who attended the swimming pool during the months of June, July, and August was

A. 80,242 B. 93,256 C. 133,843 D. 210,382

Questions 15-22.

DIRECTIONS: Questions 15 through 22 test how well you understand what you read. It will be necessary for you to read carefully because your answers to these questions must be based ONLY on the information in the following paragraphs.

The telephone directory is made up of two books. The first book consists of the introductory section and the alphabetical listing of names section. The second book is the classified directory (also known as the yellow pages). Many people who are familiar with one book do not realize how useful the other can be. The efficient office worker should become familiar with both books in order to make the best use of this important source of information.

The introductory section gives general instructions for finding numbers in the alphabetical listing and classified directory. This section also explains how to use the telephone company's many services, including the operator and information services, gives examples of charges for local and long-distance calls, and lists area codes for the entire country. In addition, this section provides a useful postal zip code map.

The alphabetical listing of names section lists the names, addresses, and telephone numbers of subscribers in an area. Guide names, or *telltales,* are on the top corner of each page. These guide names indicate the first and last name to be found on that page. *Telltales* help locate any particular name quickly. A cross-reference spelling is also given to help locate names which are spelled several different ways. City, state, and federal government agencies are listed under the major government heading. For example, an agency of the federal government would be listed under *United States Government.*

The classified directory, or yellow pages, is a separate book. In this section are advertising services, public transportation line maps, shopping guides, and listings of businesses arranged by the type of product or services they offer. This book is most useful when looking for the name or phone number of a business when all that is known is the type of product offered and the address, or when trying to locate a particular type of business in an area. Businesses listed in the classified directory can usually be found in the alphabetical listing of names section. When the name of the business is known, you will find the address or phone number more quickly in the alphabetical listing of names section.

15. The introductory section provides 15.____

A. shopping guides B. government listings
C. business listings D. information services

16. Advertising services would be found in the 16.____

A. introductory section B. alphabetical listing of names section
C. classified directory D. information services

17. According to the information in the above passage for locating government agencies, the Information Office of the Department of Consumer Affairs of New York City government would be alphabetically listed FIRST under 17.____

A. *I* for Information Offices
B. *D* for Department of Consumer Affairs
C. *N* for New York City
D. *G* for government

18. When the name of a business is known, the QUICKEST way to find the phone number is to look in the 18.____

A. classified directory
B. introductory section
C. alphabetical listing of names section
D. advertising service section

19. The QUICKEST way to find the phone number of a business when the type of service a business offers and its address is known is to look in the 19.____

A. classified directory
B. alphabetical listing of names section
C. introductory section
D. information service

20. What is a *telltale?* 20.____

A. An alphabetical listing
B. A guide name
C. A map
D. A cross-reference listing

21. The BEST way to find a postal zip code is to look in the 21.____

A. classified directory
B. introductory section
C. alphabetical listing of names section
D. government heading

22. To help find names which have several different spellings, the telephone directory provides 22.____

A. cross-reference spelling
B. *telltales*
C. spelling guides
D. advertising services

23. Assume that your agency has been given $2025 to purchase file cabinets.
If each file cabinet costs $135, how many file cabinets can your agency purchase? 23.____

A. 8
B. 10
C. 15
D. 16

24. Assume that your unit ordered 14 staplers at a total cost of $30.20, and each stapler cost the same. 24.____
The cost of one stapler was MOST NEARLY

A. $1.02 B. $1.61 C. $2.16 D. $2.26

25. Assume that you are responsible for counting and recording licensing fees collected by your department. On a particular day, your department collected in fees 40 checks in the amount of $6 each, 80 checks in the amount of $4 each, 45 twenty dollar bills, 30 ten dollar bills, 42 five dollar bills, and 186 one dollar bills. 25.____
The TOTAL amount in fees collected on that day was

A. $1,406 B. $1,706 C. $2,156 D. $2,356

26. Assume that you are responsible for your agency's petty cash fund. During the month of February, you pay out 7 $2.00 subway fares and one taxi fare for $10.85. You pay out nothing else from the fund. At the end of February, you count the money left in the fund and find 3 one dollar bills, 4 quarters, 5 dimes, and 4 nickels. The amount of money you had available in the petty cash fund at the BEGINNING of February was 26.____

A. $4.70 B. $16.35 C. $24.85 D. $29.55

27. You overhear your supervisor criticize a co-worker for handling equipment in an unsafe way. You feel that the criticism may be unfair. 27.____
Of the following, it would be BEST for you to

A. take your co-worker aside and tell her how you feel about your supervisor's comments
B. interrupt the discussion and defend your co-worker to your supervisor
C. continue working as if you had not overheard the discussion
D. make a list of other workers who have violated safety rules and give it to your supervisor

28. Assume that you have been assigned to work on a long-term project with an employee who is known for being uncooperative. 28.____
In beginning to work with this employee, it would be LEAST desirable for you to

A. understand why the person is uncooperative
B. act in a calm manner rather than an emotional manner
C. be appreciative of the co-worker's work
D. report the co-worker's lack of cooperation to your supervisor

29. Assume that you are assigned to sell tickets at a city-owned ice skating rink. An adult ticket costs $4.50, and a children's ticket costs $2.25. At the end of a day, you find that you have sold 36 adult tickets and 80 children's tickets. 29.____
The TOTAL amount of money you collected for that day was

A. $244.80 B. $318.00 C. $342.00 D. $348.00

30. If each office worker files 487 index cards in one hour, how many cards can 26 office workers file in one hour? 30.____

A. 10,662 B. 12,175 C. 12,662 D. 14,266

KEY (CORRECT ANSWERS)

1. D
2. B
3. A
4. D
5. A

6. A
7. C
8. B
9. A
10. C

11. C
12. D
13. A
14. C
15. D

16. C
17. C
18. C
19. A
20. B

21. B
22. A
23. C
24. C
25. C

26. D
27. C
28. D
29. C
30. C

EXAMINATION SECTION
TEST 1

DIRECTIONS: Each question or incomplete statement is followed by several suggested answers or completions. Select the one that BEST answers the question or completes the statement. *PRINT THE LETTER OF THE CORRECT ANSWER IN THE SPACE AT THE RIGHT.*

1. Assume that a few co-workers meet near your desk and talk about personal matters during working hours. Lately, this practice has interfered with your work. In order to stop this practice, the BEST action for you to take FIRST is to 1.____

   A. ask your supervisor to put a stop to the co-workers' meeting near your desk
   B. discontinue any friendship with this group
   C. ask your co-workers not to meet near your desk
   D. request that your desk be moved to another location

2. In order to maintain office coverage during working hours, your supervisor has scheduled your lunch hour from 1 P.M. to 2 P.M. and your co-worker's lunch hour from 12 P.M. to 1 P.M. Lately, your co-worker has been returning late from lunch each day. As a result, you don't get a full hour since you must return to the office by 2 P.M. Of the following, the BEST action for you to take FIRST is to 2.____

   A. explain to your co-worker in a courteous manner that his lateness is interfering with your right to a full hour for lunch
   B. tell your co-worker that his lateness must stop or you will report him to your supervisor
   C. report your co-worker's lateness to your supervisor
   D. leave at 1 P.M. for lunch, whether your co-worker has returned or not

3. Assume that, as an office worker, one of your jobs is to open mail sent to your unit, read the mail for content, and send the mail to the appropriate person to handle. You accidentally open and begin to read a letter marked *personal* addressed to a co-worker. Of the following, the BEST action for you to take is to 3.____

   A. report to your supervisor that your co-worker is receiving personal mail at the office
   B. destroy the letter so that your co-worker does not know you saw it
   C. reseal the letter and place it on the co-worker's desk without saying anything
   D. bring the letter to your co-worker and explain that you opened it by accident

4. Suppose that in evaluating your work, your supervisor gives you an overall good rating, but states that you sometimes turn in work with careless errors. The BEST action for you to take would be to 4.____

   A. ask a co-worker who is good at details to proofread your work
   B. take time to do a careful job, paying more attention to detail
   C. continue working as usual since occasional errors are to be expected
   D. ask your supervisor if she would mind correcting your errors

5. Assume that you are taking a telephone message for a co-worker who is not in the office at the time. Of the following, the LEAST important item to write on the message is the 5.____

   A. length of the call
   B. name of the caller
   C. time of the call
   D. telephone number of the caller

Questions 6-13.

DIRECTIONS: Questions 6 through 13 each consist of a sentence which may or may not be an example of good English. The underlined parts of each sentence may be correct or incorrect. Examine each sentence, considering grammar, punctuation, spelling, and capitalization. If the English usage in the underlined parts of the sentence given is better than any of the changes in the underlined words suggested in Options B, C, or D, choose Option A. If the changes in the underlined words suggested in Options B, C, or D would make the sentence correct, choose the correct option. Do not choose an option that will change the meaning of the sentence.

6. This Fall, the office will be closed on Columbus Day, October 9th. 6.____

A. Correct as is
B. fall...Columbus Day, October
C. Fall...columbus day, October
D. fall...Columbus Day, october

7. This manual discribes the duties performed by an Office Aide. 7.____

A. Correct as is
B. describe the duties performed
C. discribe the duties performed
D. describes the duties performed

8. There weren't no paper in the supply closet. 8.____

A. Correct as is
B. weren't any
C. wasn't any
D. wasn't no

9. The new employees left there office to attend a meeting. 9.____

A. Correct as is
B. they're
C. their
D. thier

10. The office worker started working at 8;30 a.m. 10.____

A. Correct as is
B. 8:30 a.m.
C. 8;30 a,m.
D. 8:30 am.

11. The alphabet, or A to Z sequence are the basis of most filing systems. 11.____

A. Correct as is
B. alphabet, or A to Z sequence, is
C. alphabet, or A to Z sequence are
D. alphabet, or A too Z sequence, is

12. Those file cabinets are five feet tall. 12.____

A. Correct as is
B. Them...feet
C. Those...foot
D. Them...foot

13. The Office Aide checked the reqister and finding the dato of thc meeting. 13.____

A. Correct as is
B. regaster and finding
C. register and found
D. regaster and found

Questions 14-21.

DIRECTIONS: Each of Questions 14 through 21 has two lists of numbers. Each list contains three sets of numbers. Check each of the three sets in the list on the right to see if they are the same as the corresponding set in the list on the left. Mark your answers:

A. If none of the sets in the right list are the same as those in the left list
B. if only one of the sets in the right list are the same as those in the left list
C. if only two of the sets in the right list are the same as those in the left list
D. if all three sets in the right list are the same as those in the left list

14.	7354183476 4474747744 57914302311	7354983476 4474747774 57914302311	14.____
15.	7143592185 8344517699 9178531263	7143892185 8344518699 9178531263	15.____
16.	2572114731 8806835476 8255831246	257214731 8806835476 8255831246	16.____
17.	331476853821 6976658532996 3766042113715	331476858621 6976655832996 3766042113745	17.____
18.	8806663315 74477138449 211756663666	8806663315 74477138449 211756663666	18.____
19.	990006966996 53022219743 4171171117717	99000696996 53022219843 4171171177717	19.____
20.	24400222433004 5300030055000355 20000075532002022	24400222433004 5300030055500355 20000075532002022	20.____
21.	611166640660001116 7111300117001100733 26666446664476518	61116664066001116 7111300117001100733 26666446664476518	21.____

Questions 22-25.

DIRECTIONS: Each of Questions 22 through 25 has two lists of names and addresses. Each list contains three sets of names and addresses. Check each of the three sets in the list on the right to see if they are the same as the corresponding set in the list on the left. Mark your answers:

A. if none of the sets in the right list are the same as those in the left list
B. if only one of the sets in the right list is the same as those in the left list
C. if only two of the sets in the right list are the same as those in the left list
D. if all three sets in the right list are the same as those in the left list

22.	Mary T. Berlinger 2351 Hampton St. Monsey, N.Y. 20117	Mary T. Berlinger 2351 Hampton St. Monsey, N.Y. 20117	22.____
	Eduardo Benes 473 Kingston Avenue Central Islip, N.Y. 11734	Eduardo Benes 473 Kingston Avenue Central Islip, N.Y. 11734	
	Alan Carrington Fuchs 17 Gnarled Hollow Road Los Angeles, CA 91635	Alan Carrington Fuchs 17 Gnarled Hollow Road Los Angeles, CA 91685	
23.	David John Jacobson 178 35 St. Apt. 4C New York, N.Y. 00927	David John Jacobson 178 53 St. Apt. 4C New York, N.Y. 00927	23.____
	Ann-Marie Calonella 7243 South Ridge Blvd. Bakersfield, CA 96714	Ann-Marie Calonella 7243 South Ridge Blvd. Bakersfield, CA 96714	
	Pauline M. Thompson 872 Linden Ave. Houston, Texas 70321	Pauline M. Thomson 872 Linden Ave. Houston, Texas 70321	
24.	Chester LeRoy Masterton 152 Lacy Rd. Kankakee, Ill. 54532	Chester LeRoy Masterson 152 Lacy Rd. Kankakee, Ill. 54532	24.____
	William Maloney S. LaCrosse Pla. Wausau, Wisconsin 52146	William Maloney S. LaCross Pla. Wausau, Wisconsin 52146	
	Cynthia V. Barnes 16 Pines Rd. Greenpoint, Miss. 20376	Cynthia V. Barnes 16 Pines Rd. Greenpoint, Miss. 20376	

25.	Marcel Jean Frontenac 6 Burton On The Water Calender, Me. 01471	Marcel Jean Frontenac 6 Burton On The Water Calender, Me. 01471	25.____
	J. Scott Marsden 174 S. Tipton St. Cleveland, Ohio	J. Scott Marsden 174 Tipton St. Cleveland, Ohio	
	Lawrence T. Haney 171 McDonough St. Decatur, Ga. 31304	Lawrence T. Haney 171 McDonough St. Decatur, Ga. 31304	

KEY (CORRECT ANSWERS)

1. C
2. A
3. D
4. B
5. A
6. A
7. D
8. C
9. C
10. B
11. B
12. A
13. C
14. B
15. B
16. C
17. A
18. D
19. A
20. C
21. C
22. C
23. B
24. B
25. C

TEST 2

DIRECTIONS: Each question or incomplete statement is followed by several suggested answers or completions. Select the one that BEST answers the question or completes the statement. *PRINT THE LETTER OF THE CORRECT ANSWER IN THE SPACE AT THE RIGHT.*

Questions 1-6.

DIRECTIONS: Questions 1 through 6 are to be answered SOLELY on the basis of the information contained in the following passage.

Duplicating is the process of making a number of identical copies of letters, documents, etc. from an original. Some duplicating processes make copies directly from the original document. Other duplicating processes require the preparation of a special master, and copies are then made from the master. Four of the most common duplicating processes are stencil, fluid, offset, and xerox.

In the stencil process, the typewriter is used to cut the words into a master called a stencil. Drawings, charts, or graphs can be cut into the stencil using a stylus. As many as 3,500 good-quality copies can be reproduced from one stencil. Various grades of finished paper from inexpensive mimeograph to expensive bond can be used.

The fluid process is a good method of copying from 50 to 125 good-quality copies from a master, which is prepared with a special dye. The master is placed on the duplicator, and special paper with a hard finish is moistened and then passed through the duplicator. Some of the dye on the master is dissolved, creating an impression on the paper. The impression becomes lighter as more copies are made; and once the dye on the master is used up, a new master must be made.

The offset process is the most adaptable office duplicating process because this process can be used for making a few copies or many copies. Masters can be made on paper or plastic for a few hundred copies, or on metal plates for as many as 75,000 copies. By using a special technique called photo-offset, charts, photographs, illustrations, or graphs can be reproduced on the master plate. The offset process is capable of producing large quantities of fine, top-quality copies on all types of finished paper.

The xerox process reproduces an exact duplicate from an original. It is the fastest duplicating method because the original material is placed directly on the duplicator, eliminating the need to make a special master. Any kind of paper can be used. The xerox process is the most expensive duplicating process; however, it is the best method of reproducing small quantities of good-quality copies of reports, letters, official documents, memos, or contracts.

1. Of the following, the MOST efficient method of reproducing 5,000 copies of a graph is 1.____

   A. stencil B. fluid C. offset D. xerox

2. The offset process is the MOST adaptable office duplicating process because 2.____

   A. it is the quickest duplicating method
   B. it is the least expensive duplicating method
   C. it can produce a small number or large number of copies
   D. a softer master can be used over and over again

3. Which one of the following duplicating processes uses moistened paper? 3.____

A. Stencil B. Fluid C. Offset D. Xerox

4. The fluid process would be the BEST process to use for reproducing 4.____

A. five copies of a school transcript
B. fifty copies of a memo
C. five hundred copies of a form letter
D. five thousand copies of a chart

5. Which one of the following duplicating processes does NOT require a special master? 5.____

A. Fluid B. Xerox C. Offset D. Stencil

6. Xerox is NOT used for all duplicating jobs because 6.____

A. it produces poor-quality copies
B. the process is too expensive
C. preparing the master is too time-consuming
D. it cannot produce written reports

7. Assume a city agency has 775 office workers. 7.____
If 2 out of 25 office workers were absent on a particular day, how many office workers reported to work on that day?

A. 713 B. 744 C. 750 D. 773

Questions 8-11.

DIRECTIONS: In Questions 8 through 11, select the choice that is CLOSEST in meaning to the underlined word.

SAMPLE: This division reviews the <u>fiscal</u> reports of the agency.
In this sentence, the word <u>fiscal</u> means MOST NEARLY
A. financial B. critical C. basic D. personnel

The correct answer is A, financial, because financial is closest to <u>fiscal</u>.

8. A central file eliminates the need to <u>retain</u> duplicate material. 8.____
The word <u>retain</u> means MOST NEARLY

A. keep B. change C. locate D. process

9. Filing is a <u>routine</u> office task. 9.____
<u>Routine</u> means MOST NEARLY

A. proper B. regular C. simple D. difficult

10. Sometimes a word, phrase, or sentence must be <u>deleted</u> to correct an error. 10.____
<u>Deleted</u> means MOST NEARLY

A. removed B. added C. expanded D. improved

11. Your supervisor will evaluate your work. 11.____
Evaluate means MOST NEARLY

A. judge B. list C. assign D. explain

Questions 12-19.

DIRECTIONS: The code table below shows 10 letters with matching numbers. For each Question 12 through 19, there are three sets of letters. Each set of letters is followed by a set of numbers which may or may not match their correct letter according to the code table. For each question, check all three sets of letters and numbers and mark your answer:
A. if no pairs are correctly matched
B. if only one pair is correctly matched
C. if only two pairs are correctly matched
D. if all three pairs are correctly matched

CODE TABLE

T	M	V	D	S	P	R	G	B	H
1	2	3	4	5	6	7	8	9	0

Sample Question: TMVDSP - 123456
RGBHTM - 789011
DSPRGB - 256789

In the sample question above, the first set of numbers correctly matches its set of letters. But the second and third pairs contain mistakes. In the second pair, M is incorrectly matched with number 1. According to the code table, letter M should be correctly matched with number 2. In the third pair, the letter D is incorrectly matched with number 2. According to the code table, letter D should be correctly matched with number 4. Since only one of the pairs is correctly matched, the answer to this sample question is B.

12. RSBMRM - 759262 12.____
GDSRVH - 845730
VDBRTM - 349713

13. TGVSDR - 183247 13.____
SMHRDP - 520647
TRMHSR - 172057

14. DSPRGM - 456782 14.____
MVDBHT - 234902
HPMDBT - 062491

15. BVPTRD - 936184 15.____
GDPHMB - 807029
GMRHMV - 827032

16. MGVRSH - 283750 16.____
TRDMBS - 174295
SPRMGV - 567283

17. SGBSDM - 489542 17.____
MGHPTM - 290612
MPBMHT - 269301

18. TDPBHM - 146902 18.____
VPBMRS - 369275
GDMBHM - 842902

19. MVPTBV - 236194 19.____
PDRTMB - 647128
BGTMSM - 981232

Questions 20-25.

DIRECTIONS: In each of Questions 20 through 25, the names of four people are given. For each question, choose as your answer the one of the four names given which should be filed FIRST according to the usual system of alphabetical filing of names, as described in the following paragraph.

In filing names, you must start with the last name. Names are filed in order of the first letter of the last name, then the second letter, etc. Therefore, BAILY would be filed before BROWN, which would be filed before COLT. A name with fewer letters of the same type comes first; i.e., Smith before Smithe. If the last names are the same, the names are filed alphabetically by the first name. If the first name is an initial, a name with an initial would come before a first name that starts with the same letter as the initial. Therefore, I. BROWN would come before IRA BROWN. Finally, if both last name and first name are the same, the name would be filed alphabetically by the middle name, one again an initial coming before a middle name which starts with the same letter as the initial. If there is no middle name at all, the name would come before those with middle initials or names.

Sample Question: A. Lester Daniels
B. William Dancer
C. Nathan Danzig
D. Dan Lester

The last names beginning with D are filed before the last name beginning with L. Since DANIELS, DANCER, and DANZIG all begin with the same three letters, you must look at the fourth letter of the last name to determine which name should be filed first. C comes before I or Z in the alphabet, so DANCER is filed before DANIELS or DANZIG. Therefore, the answer to the above sample question is B.

20. A. Scott Biala B. Mary Byala 20.____
C. Martin Baylor D. Francis Bauer

21. A. Howard J. Black B. Howard Black 21.____
C. J. Howard Black D. John H. Black

22. A. Theodora Garth Kingston B. Theadore Barth Kingston 22.____
C. Thomas Kingston D. Thomas T. Kingston

23. A. Paulette Mary Huerta B. Paul M. Huerta 23.____
C. Paulette L. Huerta D. Peter A. Huerta

24. A. Martha Hunt Morgan B. Martin Hunt Morgan 24.____
C. Mary H. Morgan D. Martine H. Morgan

25. A. James T. Meerschaum B. James M. Mershum 25.____
C. James F. Mearshaum D. James N. Meshum

KEY (CORRECT ANSWERS)

1.	C	11.	A
2.	C	12.	B
3.	B	13.	B
4.	B	14.	C
5.	B	15.	A
6.	B	16.	D
7.	A	17.	A
8.	A	18.	D
9.	B	19.	A
10.	A	20.	D

21.	B
22.	B
23.	B
24.	A
25.	C

TEST 3

DIRECTIONS: Each question or incomplete statement is followed by several suggested answers or completions. Select the one that BEST answers the question or completes the statement. *PRINT THE LETTER OF THE CORRECT ANSWER IN THE SPACE AT THE RIGHT.*

1. Which one of the following statements about proper telephone usage is NOT always correct? 1.____
When answering the telephone, you should

   A. know whom you are speaking to
   B. give the caller your undivided attention
   C. identify yourself to the caller
   D. obtain the information the caller wishes before you do your other work

2. Assume that, as a member of a worker's safety committee in your agency, you are responsible for encouraging other employees to follow correct safety practices. While you are working on your regular assignment, you observe an employee violating a safety rule. 2.____
Of the following, the BEST action for you to take FIRST is to

   A. speak to the employee about safety practices and order him to stop violating the safety rule
   B. speak to the employee about safety practices and point out the safety rule he is violating
   C. bring the matter up in the next committee meeting
   D. report this violation of the safety rule to the employee's supervisor

3. Assume that you have been temporarily assigned by your supervisor to do a job which you do not want to do. The BEST action for you to take is to 3.____

   A. discuss the job with your supervisor, explaining why you do not want to do it
   B. discuss the job with your supervisor and tell her that you will not do it
   C. ask a co-worker to take your place on this job
   D. do some other job that you like; your supervisor may give the job you do not like to someone else

4. Assume that you keep the confidential personnel files of employees in your unit. A friend asks you to obtain some information from the file of one of your co-workers. 4.____
The BEST action to take is to ______ to your friend.

   A. ask the co-worker if you can give the information
   B. ask your supervisor if you can give the information
   C. give the information
   D. refuse to give the information

Questions 5-8.

DIRECTIONS: Questions 5 through 8 are to be answered SOLELY on the basis of the information contained in the following passage.

City government is committed to providing a safe and healthy work environment for all city employees. An effective agency safety program reduces accidents by educating employees about the types of careless acts which can cause accidents. Even in an office, accidents can happen. If each employee is aware of possible safety hazards, the number of accidents on the job can be reduced.

Careless use of office equipment can cause accidents and injuries. For example, file cabinet drawers which are filled with papers can be so heavy that the entire cabinet could tip over from the weight of one open drawer.

The bottom drawers of desks and file cabinets should never be left open since employees could easily trip over open drawers and injure themselves.

When reaching for objects on a high shelf, an employee should use a strong, sturdy object such as a step stool to stand on. Makeshift platforms made out of books, papers, or boxes can easily collapse. Even chairs can slide out from under foot, causing serious injury.

Even at an employee's desk, safety hazards can occur. Frayed or cut wires should be repaired or replaced immediately. Computers which are not firmly anchored to the desk or table could fall, causing injury.

Smoking is one of the major causes of fires in the office. A lighted match or improperly extinguished cigarette thrown into a wastebasket filled with paper could cause a major fire with possible loss of life. Where smoking is permitted, ashtrays should be used. Smoking is particularly dangerous in offices where flammable chemicals are used.

5. The goal of an effective safety program is to 5.____

A. reduce office accidents
B. stop employees from smoking on the job
C. encourage employees to continue their education
D. eliminate high shelves in offices

6. Desks and file cabinets can become safety hazards when 6.____

A. their drawers are left open
B. they are used as wastebaskets
C. they are makeshift
D. they are not anchored securely to the floor

7. Smoking is especially hazardous when it occurs 7.____

A. near exposed wires
B. in a crowded office
C. in an area where flammable chemicals are used
D. where books and papers are stored

8. Accidents are likely to occur when 8.____

A. employees' desks are cluttered with books and papers
B. employees are not aware of safety hazards
C. employees close desk drawers
D. step stools are used to reach high objects

9. Assume that part of your job as a worker in the accounting division of a city agency is to answer the telephone. When you first answer the telephone, it is LEAST important to tell the caller 9.____

A. your title
B. your name
C. the name of your unit
D. the name of your agency

10. Assume that you are assigned to work as a receptionist, and your duties are to answer phones, greet visitors, and do other general office work. You are busy with a routine job when several visitors approach your desk. 10.____
The BEST action to take is to

A. ask the visitors to have a seat and assist them after your work is completed
B. tell the visitors that you are busy and they should return at a more convenient time
C. stop working long enough to assist the visitors
D. continue working and wait for the visitors to ask you for assistance

11. Assume that your supervisor has chosen you to take a special course during working hours to learn a new payroll procedure. Although you know that you were chosen because of your good work record, a co-worker, who feels that he should have been chosen, has been telling everyone in your unit that the choice was unfair. 11.____
Of the following, the BEST way to handle this situation FIRST is to

A. suggest to the co-worker that everything in life is unfair
B. contact your union representative in case your co-worker presents a formal grievance
C. tell your supervisor about your co-worker's complaints and let her handle the situation
D. tell the co-worker that you were chosen because of your superior work record

12. Assume that while you are working on an assignment which must be completed quickly, a supervisor from another unit asks you to obtain information for her. 12.____
Of the following, the BEST way to respond to her request is to

A. tell her to return in an hour since you are busy
B. give her the names of some people in her own unit who could help her
C. tell her you are busy and refer her to a co-worker
D. tell her that you are busy and ask her if she could wait until you finish your assignment

13. A co-worker in your unit is often off from work because of illness. Your supervisor assigns the co-worker's work to you when she is not there. Lately, doing her work has interfered with your own job. 13.____
The BEST action for you to take FIRST is to

A. discuss the problem with your supervisor
B. complete your own work before starting your co-worker's work
C. ask other workers in your unit to assist you
D. work late in order to get the jobs done

14. During the month of June, 40,587 people attended a city-owned swimming pool. In July, 13,014 more people attended the swimming pool than the number that had attended in June. In August, 39,655 people attended the swimming pool. 14.____
The TOTAL number of people who attended the swimming pool during the months of June, July, and August was

A. 80,242 B. 93,256 C. 133,843 D. 210,382

Questions 15-22.

DIRECTIONS: Questions 15 through 22 test how well you understand what you read. It will be necessary for you to read carefully because your answers to these questions must be based ONLY on the information in the following paragraphs.

The telephone directory is made up of two books. The first book consists of the introductory section and the alphabetical listing of names section. The second book is the classified directory (also known as the yellow pages). Many people who are familiar with one book do not realize how useful the other can be. The efficient office worker should become familiar with both books in order to make the best use of this important source of information.

The introductory section gives general instructions for finding numbers in the alphabetical listing and classified directory. This section also explains how to use the telephone company's many services, including the operator and information services, gives examples of charges for local and long-distance calls, and lists area codes for the entire country. In addition, this section provides a useful postal zip code map.

The alphabetical listing of names section lists the names, addresses, and telephone numbers of subscribers in an area. Guide names, or *telltales,* are on the top corner of each page. These guide names indicate the first and last name to be found on that page. *Telltales* help locate any particular name quickly. A cross-reference spelling is also given to help locate names which are spelled several different ways. City, state, and federal government agencies are listed under the major government heading. For example, an agency of the federal government would be listed under *United States Government.*

The classified directory, or yellow pages, is a separate book. In this section are advertising services, public transportation line maps, shopping guides, and listings of businesses arranged by the type of product or services they offer. This book is most useful when looking for the name or phone number of a business when all that is known is the type of product offered and the address, or when trying to locate a particular type of business in an area. Businesses listed in the classified directory can usually be found in the alphabetical listing of names section. When the name of the business is known, you will find the address or phone number more quickly in the alphabetical listing of names section.

15. The introductory section provides 15.____

A. shopping guides
B. government listings
C. business listings
D. information services

16. Advertising services would be found in the 16.____

A. introductory section
B. alphabetical listing of names section
C. classified directory
D. information services

17. According to the information in the above passage for locating government agencies, the Information Office of the Department of Consumer Affairs of New York City government would be alphabetically listed FIRST under 17.____

A. *I* for Information Offices
B. *D* for Department of Consumer Affairs
C. *N* for New York City
D. *G* for government

18. When the name of a business is known, the QUICKEST way to find the phone number is to look in the 18.____

A. classified directory
B. introductory section
C. alphabetical listing of names section
D. advertising service section

19. The QUICKEST way to find the phone number of a business when the type of service a business offers and its address is known is to look in the 19.____

A. classified directory
B. alphabetical listing of names section
C. introductory section
D. information service

20. What is a *telltale?* 20.____

A. An alphabetical listing
B. A guide name
C. A map
D. A cross-reference listing

21. The BEST way to find a postal zip code is to look in the 21.____

A. classified directory
B. introductory section
C. alphabetical listing of names section
D. government heading

22. To help find names which have several different spellings, the telephone directory provides 22.____

A. cross-reference spelling
B. *telltales*
C. spelling guides
D. advertising services

23. Assume that your agency has been given $2025 to purchase file cabinets. If each file cabinet costs $135, how many file cabinets can your agency purchase? 23.____

A. 8
B. 10
C. 15
D. 16

24. Assume that your unit ordered 14 staplers at a total cost of $30.20, and each stapler cost the same. 24.____
The cost of one stapler was MOST NEARLY

A. $1.02 B. $1.61 C. $2.16 D. $2.26

25. Assume that you are responsible for counting and recording licensing fees collected by your department. On a particular day, your department collected in fees 40 checks in the amount of $6 each, 80 checks in the amount of $4 each, 45 twenty dollar bills, 30 ten dollar bills, 42 five dollar bills, and 186 one dollar bills. 25.____
The TOTAL amount in fees collected on that day was

A. $1,406 B. $1,706 C. $2,156 D. $2,356

26. Assume that you are responsible for your agency's petty cash fund. During the month of February, you pay out 7 $2.00 subway fares and one taxi fare for $10.85. You pay out nothing else from the fund. At the end of February, you count the money left in the fund and find 3 one dollar bills, 4 quarters, 5 dimes, and 4 nickels. The amount of money you had available in the petty cash fund at the BEGINNING of February was 26.____

A. $4.70 B. $16.35 C. $24.85 D. $29.55

27. You overhear your supervisor criticize a co-worker for handling equipment in an unsafe way. You feel that the criticism may be unfair. 27.____
Of the following, it would be BEST for you to

A. take your co-worker aside and tell her how you feel about your supervisor's comments
B. interrupt the discussion and defend your co-worker to your supervisor
C. continue working as if you had not overheard the discussion
D. make a list of other workers who have violated safety rules and give it to your supervisor

28. Assume that you have been assigned to work on a long-term project with an employee who is known for being uncooperative. 28.____
In beginning to work with this employee, it would be LEAST desirable for you to

A. understand why the person is uncooperative
B. act in a calm manner rather than an emotional manner
C. be appreciative of the co-worker's work
D. report the co-worker's lack of cooperation to your supervisor

29. Assume that you are assigned to sell tickets at a city-owned ice skating rink. An adult ticket costs $4.50, and a children's ticket costs $2.25. At the end of a day, you find that you have sold 36 adult tickets and 80 children's tickets. 29.____
The TOTAL amount of money you collected for that day was

A. $244.80 B. $318.00 C. $342.00 D. $348.00

30. If each office worker files 487 index cards in one hour, how many cards can 26 office workers file in one hour? 30.____

A. 10,662 B. 12,175 C. 12,662 D. 14,266

KEY (CORRECT ANSWERS)

1.	D	16.	C
2.	B	17.	C
3.	A	18.	C
4.	D	19.	A
5.	A	20.	B
6.	A	21.	B
7.	C	22.	A
8.	B	23.	C
9.	A	24.	C
10.	C	25.	C
11.	C	26.	D
12.	D	27.	C
13.	A	28.	D
14.	C	29.	C
15.	D	30.	C

EXAMINATION SECTION
TEST 1

DIRECTIONS: Each question or incomplete statement is followed by several suggested answers or completions. Select the one that BEST answers the question or completes the statement. *PRINT THE LETTER OF THE CORRECT ANSWER IN THE SPACE AT THE RIGHT.*

1. In considering a new word processing system for a regional office, which of the following would MOST likely be the MOST important consideration in making a decision? 1.____

   A. Ease of operation
   B. Friendliness of service technicians
   C. Availability of service technicians
   D. Capacity of the system to meet the unit's word processing needs

2. Your supervisor is out of town for several days and has asked you to act as supervisor in his absence. An employee in the unit comes to you and complains that the supervisor has been dividing the workload unfairly. 2.____
   Of the following, the MOST appropriate action for you to take is

   A. defend the actions of your supervisor
   B. encourage the employee to file a grievance
   C. listen to the employee attentively
   D. explain to the employee that you have no authority to handle the situation

3. A principal stenographer still on probation is instructed to supervise and coordinate the completion of a large word processing project. Her supervisor asks her how long she thinks the project will take. The principal stenographer gives her supervisor an estimate that is two days longer than she actually thinks the project will take to complete. The project is completed two days earlier, and the principal stenographer is congratulated by her supervisor for her efforts. 3.____
   In purposely overestimating the time required to complete the project, the principal stenographer showed

   A. *good* judgment because it helped her appear very efficient
   B. *good* judgment because it helps keep unrealistic supervisors from expecting too much
   C. *poor* judgment because plans and schedules of other components of the project may have been based on her false estimate
   D. *poor* judgment because she should have used the extra time to further check and, proofread the work

4. Which of the following would MOST likely be the MOST important in providing support to one's supervisor? 4.____

   A. Screening annoying phone calls
   B. Reviewing and forwarding articles and publications that may be of interest to your supervisor
   C. Correctly transmitting instructions from the supervisor to appropriate staff members
   D. Reviewing outgoing correspondence for proper grammatical usage and clarity

5. While you are on the telephone answering a question about your agency, a visitor comes to your desk and starts to ask you a question. There is no emergency or urgency in either situation, that of the phone call or that of answering the visitor's question. In this case, you should 5.____

   A. excuse yourself to the person on the telephone and tell the visitor that you will be with him or her as soon as you have finished on the phone
   B. explain to the person on the phone that you have a visitor and must shorten the conversation
   C. continue to talk with the person on the phone while looking up occasionally at the visitor to let him or her know that you know he or she is there
   D. continue to talk with the person on the telephone until you are finished and then let the visitor know that you're sorry to have kept him or her waiting

6. Your supervisor is out of town on vacation for one week, and asks you to act as supervisor in her absence. The second day she is gone a very important, complex budgetary form, which must be responded to in ten days, arrives in your unit. Of the following, it would be BEST if you 6.____

   A. filled out the form and submitted it as soon as possible
   B. read the form over, did any time-consuming research that might be needed, and then gave the uncompleted form to your supervisor as soon as she returned
   C. asked for help from your supervisor's supervisor in completing the form
   D. tried to contact your supervisor for advice

7. Of the following, which would MOST likely be of the highest priority? The typing of 7.____

   A. a grant proposal due next week
   B. new addresses onto a mailing list for a future mailing
   C. a payroll form for a new employee that needs to be submitted immediately
   D. a memorandum from the Commissioner to all employees regarding new procedures

8. Your office is moving to a new location. Of the following, it would be MOST important to ensure that 8.____

   A. others will know your office's new address and phone number
   B. the new office space is comfortable
   C. your supervisor is happy with his or her new office space
   D. the move itself goes smoothly

9. Of the following, which would generally be considered the LEAST desirable? 9.____

   A. Accidentally disconnecting an executive from an important phone call
   B. Ordering the wrong back-up part for a copying machine
   C. Misplacing several hundred dollars worth of personal checks payable to your department
   D. Misplacing a memorandum that needs to be typed

10. Your supervisor has told you not to let anyone disturb her for the rest of the morning unless absolutely necessary because she has some urgent work to complete. The department head telephones and asks to speak to her. The BEST course of action for you to take is to 10.____

A. ask the department head if he or she can leave a message
B. ask your supervisor if she can take the call
C. tell the department head that your supervisor is out
D. let your supervisor know that her instructions have put you in a difficult position

11. Which of the following would be MOST likely to contribute to efficiency in the operation of an office? 11.____

A. A new computer system is instituted in an office.
B. The employees are paid well.
C. Procedures and practices are studied for any redundant operations.
D. A supervisor delegates work.

12. You are at work at your desk on a special project when a visitor approaches you. You cannot interrupt your work to take care of this person. Of the following, the BEST and MOST courteous way of handling this situation is to 12.____

A. avoid looking up from your work until you are finished with what you are doing
B. tell the visitor that you will not be able to assist him or her for quite some time
C. refer the individual to another employee who can take care of him or her right away
D. chat with the individual while you continue to work

13. Which of the following would MOST likely be of the highest priority? A(n) 13.____

A. annual report due next month
B. irate member of the public who is standing at your desk
C. important financial report requested by the Commissioner
D. memorandum to all employees outlining very important new policy needs to be typed and distributed immediately

14. Someone uses *special pull* to obtain the services of your unit at the last minute. You and the four employees you supervise have done everything you could do to provide good service, and you feel things have gone very well. The client is not pleased, however, and enters your office and begins screaming at you and the other employees present. Of the following, it would be BEST if you 14.____

A. ignored the person
B. tried to calm the person down
C. asked the person to leave the office
D. called your supervisor in to help handle the situation

15. Your supervisor is on vacation for two weeks, and you have been asked to fill in for her. Your office is very busy, and there is a strict procedure for filling requests. Leslie from Unit X wants something completed immediately. You don't feel this is possible or reasonable, and politely explain why to Leslie. Leslie becomes very angry and says that she will complain to your supervisor about your uncooperative behavior as soon as your supervisor returns. 15.____
Of the following, it would be BEST if you

A. filled Leslie's request
B. reported Leslie to her supervisor
C. complained to your supervisor about the situation as soon as she returned
D. stood by your decision once you determined it was correct

KEY (CORRECT ANSWERS)

1. D	6. B	11. C
2. C	7. C	12. C
3. C	8. A	13. B
4. C	9. C	14. B
5. A	10. B	15. D

EXAMINATION SECTION
TEST 1

DIRECTIONS: Each question or incomplete statement is followed by several suggested answers or completions. Select the one that BEST answers the question or completes the statement. *PRINT THE LETTER OF THE CORRECT ANSWER IN THE SPACE AT THE RIGHT.*

1. A push-button telephone with six buttons, one of which is a *hold* button, is often used when more than one outside line is needed. If you are talking on one line of this type of telephone when another call comes in, what is the procedure to follow if you want to answer the second call but keep the first call on the line? Push the 1.____

   A. *hold* button at the same time as you push the *pickup* button of the ringing line
   B. *hold* button and then push the *pickup* button of the ringing line
   C. *pickup* button of the ringing line and then push the *hold* button
   D. *pickup* button of the ringing line and push the *hold* button when you return to the original line

2. Suppose that you are asked to prepare a petty cash statement for March. The original and one copy are to go to the personnel office. One copy is to go to the fiscal office, and another copy is to go to your supervisor. The last copy is for your files. In preparing the statement and the copies, how many sheets of copy paper should you use? 2.____

   A. 3 B. 4 C. 5 D. 8

3. Which one of the following is the LEAST important advantage of putting the subject of a letter in the heading to the right of the address? It 3.____

   A. makes filing of the copy easier
   B. makes more space available in the body of the letter
   C. simplifies distribution of letters
   D. simplifies determination of the subject of the letter

4. Of the following, the MOST efficient way to put 100 copies of a one-page letter into 9 1/2" x 4 1/8" envelopes for mailing is to fold ______ into an envelope. 4.____

   A. each letter and insert it immediately after folding
   B. each letter separately until all 100 are folded; then insert each one
   C. the 100 letters two at a time, then separate them and insert each one
   D. two letters together, slip them apart, and insert each one

5. When preparing papers for filing, it is NOT desirable to 5.____

   A. smooth papers that are wrinkled
   B. use paper clips to keep related papers together in the files
   C. arrange the papers in the order in which they will be filed
   D. mend torn papers with cellophane tape

6. Of the following, the BEST reason for a clerical unit to have its own duplicating machine is that the unit 6.____

A. uses many forms which it must reproduce internally
B. must make two copies of each piece of incoming mail for a special file
C. must make seven copies of each piece of outgoing mail
D. must type 200 envelopes each month for distribution to the same offices

7. Several offices use the same photocopying machine. 7.____
If each office must pay its share of the cost of running this machine, the BEST way of determining how much of this cost should be charged to each of these offices is to

A. determine the monthly number of photocopies made by each office
B. determine the monthly number of originals submitted for photocopying by each office
C. determine the number of times per day each office uses the photocopy machine
D. divide the total cost of running the photocopy machine by the total number of offices using the machine

8. Which one of the following would it be BEST to use to indicate that a file folder has been removed from the files for temporary use in another office? 8.____
A(n)

A. cross-reference card
B. tickler file marker
C. aperture card
D. out guide

9. Which one of the following is the MOST important objective of filing? 9.____

A. Giving a secretary something to do in her spare time
B. Making it possible to locate information quickly
C. Providing a place to store unneeded documents
D. Keeping extra papers from accumulating on workers' desks

10. If a check has been made out for an incorrect amount, the BEST action for the writer of the check to take is to 10.____

A. erase the original amount and enter the correct amount
B. cross out the original amount with a single line and enter the correct amount above it
C. black out the original amount so that it cannot be read and enter the correct amount above it
D. write a new check

11. Which one of the following BEST describes the usual arrangement of a tickler file? 11.____

A. Alphabetical
B. Chronological
C. Numerical
D. Geographical

12. Which one of the following is the LEAST desirable filing practice? 12.____

A. Using staples to keep papers together
B. Filing all material without regard to date
C. Keeping a record of all materials removed from the files
D. Writing filing instructions on each paper prior to filing

13. Assume that one of your duties is to keep records of the office supplies used by your unit for the purpose of ordering new supplies when the old supplies run out. The information that will be of MOST help in letting you know when to reorder supplies is the 13.____

A. quantity issued
B. quantity received
C. quantity on hand
D. stock number

Questions 14-19.

DIRECTIONS: Questions 14 through 19 consist of sets of names and addresses. In each question, the name and address in Column II should be an exact copy of the name and address in Column I. If there is:
a mistake *only* in the name, mark your answer A;
a mistake *only* in the address, mark your answer B;
a mistake in *both* name and address, mark your answer C;
no mistake in *either* name or address, mark your answer D.

SAMPLE QUESTION

Column I	Column II
Michael Filbert 456 Reade Street New York, N.Y. 10013	Michael Filbert 645 Reade Street New York, N.Y. 10013

Since there is a mistake only in the address (the street number should be 456 instead of 645), the answer to the sample question is B.

	COLUMN I	COLUMN II	
14.	Esta Wong 141 West 68 St. New York, N.Y. 10023	Esta Wang 141 West 68 St. New York, N.Y. 10023	14.____
15.	Dr. Alberto Grosso 3475 12th Avenue Brooklyn, N.Y. 11218	Dr. Alberto Grosso 3475 12th Avenue Brooklyn, N.Y. 11218	15.____
16.	Mrs. Ruth Bortlas 482 Theresa Ct. Far Rockaway, N.Y. 11691	Ms. Ruth Bortlas 482 Theresa Ct. Far Rockaway, N.Y. 11169	16.____
17.	Mr. and Mrs. Howard Fox 2301 Sedgwick Ave. Bronx, N.Y. 10468	Mr. and Mrs. Howard Fox 231 Sedgwick Ave. Bronx, N.Y. 10468	17.____
18.	Miss Marjorie Black 223 East 23 Street New York, N.Y. 10010	Miss Margorie Black 223 East 23 Street New York, N.Y. 10010	18.____
19.	Michelle Herman 806 Valley Rd. Old Tappan, N.J. 07675	Michelle Hermann 806 Valley Dr. Old Tappan, N.J. 07675	19.____

Questions 20-25.

DIRECTIONS: Questions 20 through 25 are to be answered SOLELY on the basis of the information in the following passage.

Basic to every office is the need for proper lighting. Inadequate lighting is a familiar cause of fatigue and serves to create a somewhat dismal atmosphere in the office. One requirement of proper lighting is that it be of an appropriate intensity. Intensity is measured in foot-candles. According to the Illuminating Engineering Society of New York, for casual seeing tasks such as in reception rooms, inactive file rooms, and other service areas, it is recommended that the amount of light be 30 foot-candles. For ordinary seeing tasks such as reading and work in active file rooms and in mail rooms, the recommended lighting is 100 foot-candles. For very difficult seeing tasks such as accounting, transcribing, and business machine use, the recommended lighting is 150 foot-candles.

Lighting intensity is only one requirement. Shadows and glare are to be avoided. For example, the larger the proportion of a ceiling filled with lighting units, the more glare-free and comfortable the lighting will be. Natural lighting from windows is not too dependable because on dark wintry days, windows yield little usable light, and on sunny, summer afternoons, the glare from windows may be very distracting. Desks should not face the windows. Finally, the main lighting source ought to be overhead and to the left of the user.

20. According to the above passage, insufficient light in the office may cause 20.____

A. glare
B. shadows
C. tiredness
D. distraction

21. Based on the above passage, which of the following must be considered when planning lighting arrangements? 21.____
The

A. amount of natural light present
B. amount of work to be done
C. level of difficulty of work to be done
D. type of activity to be carried out

22. It can be inferred from the above passage that a well-coordinated lighting scheme is LIKELY to result in 22.____

A. greater employee productivity
B. elimination of light reflection
C. lower lighting cost
D. more use of natural light

23. Of the following, the BEST title for the above passage is 23.____

A. Characteristics of Light
B. Light Measurement Devices
C. Factors to Consider When Planning Lighting Systems
D. Comfort vs. Cost When Devising Lighting Arrangements

24. According to the above passage, a foot-candle is a measurement of the 24.____

A. number of bulbs used
B. strength of the light
C. contrast between glare and shadow
D. proportion of the ceiling filled with lighting units

25. According to the above passage, the number of foot-candles of light that would be needed to copy figures onto a payroll is ______ foot-candles. 25.____

A. less than 30
B. 30
C. 100
D. 150

KEY (CORRECT ANSWERS)

1. B
2. B
3. B
4. A
5. B
6. A
7. A
8. D
9. B
10. D
11. B
12. B
13. C
14. A
15. D
16. C
17. B
18. A
19. C
20. C
21. D
22. A
23. C
24. B
25. D

TEST 2

DIRECTIONS: Each question or incomplete statement is followed by several suggested answers or completions. Select the one that BEST answers the question or completes the statement. *PRINT THE LETTER OF THE CORRECT ANSWER IN THE SPACE AT THE RIGHT.*

1. Assume that a supervisor has three subordinates who perform clerical tasks. One of the employees retires and is replaced by someone who is transferred from another unit in the agency. The transferred employee tells the supervisor that she has worked as a clerical employee for two years and understands clerical operations quite well. The supervisor then assigns the transferred employee to a desk, tells the employee to begin working, and returns to his own desk. 1.____
The supervisor's action in this situation is

   A. *proper;* experienced clerical employees do not require training when they are transferred to new assignments
   B. *improper;* before the supervisor returns to his desk, he should tell the other two subordinates to watch the transferred employee perform the work
   C. *proper;* if the transferred employee makes any mistakes, she will bring them to the supervisor's attention
   D. *improper;* the supervisor should find out what clerical tasks the transferred employee has performed and give her instruction in those which are new or different

2. Assume that you are falling behind in completing your work assignments and you believe that your workload is too heavy. 2.____
Of the following, the BEST course of action for you to take FIRST is to

   A. discuss the problem with your supervisor
   B. decide which of your assignments can be postponed
   C. try to get some of your co-workers to help you out
   D. plan to take some of the work home with you in order to catch up

3. Suppose that one of the clerks under your supervision is filling in monthly personnel forms. She asks you to explain a particular personnel regulation which is related to various items on the forms. You are not thoroughly familiar with the regulation. 3.____
Of the following responses you may make, the one which will gain the MOST respect from the clerk and which is generally the MOST advisable is to

   A. tell the clerk to do the best she can and that you will check her work later
   B. inform the clerk that you are not sure of a correct explanation but suggest a procedure for her to follow
   C. give the clerk a suitable interpretation so that she will think you are familiar with all regulations
   D. tell the clerk that you will have to read the regulation more thoroughly before you can give her an explanation

4. Charging out records until a specified due date, with prompt follow-up if they are not returned, is a 4.____

A. *good* idea; it may prevent the records from being kept needlessly on someone's desk for long periods of time
B. *good* idea; it will indicate the extent of your authority to other departments
C. *poor* idea; the person borrowing the material may make an error because of the pressure put upon him to return the records
D. *poor* idea; other departments will feel that you do not trust them with the records and they will be resentful

Questions 5-9.

DIRECTIONS: Questions 5 through 9 consist of three lines of code letters and numbers. The numbers on each line should correspond with the code letters on the same line in accordance with the table below.

Code Letter	P	L	I	J	B	O	H	U	C	G
Corresponding Number	0	1	2	3	4	5	6	7	8	9

On some of the lines, an error exists in the coding. Compare the letters and numbers in each question carefully. If you find an error or errors on
only *one* of the lines in the question, mark your answer A;
any *two* lines in the question, mark your answer B;
all *three* lines in the question, mark your answer C;
none of the lines in the question, mark your answer D.

<u>SAMPLE QUESTION</u>

JHOILCP 3652180
BICLGUP 4286970
UCIBHLJ 5824613

In the above sample, the first line is correct since each code letter listed has the correct corresponding number. On the second line, an error exists because code letter L should have the number 1 instead of the number 6. On the third line, an error exists because the code letter U should have the number 7 instead of the number 5. Since there are errors on two of the three lines, the correct answer is B.

5. BULJCIP 4713920 5.____
HIGPOUL 6290571
OCUHJBI 5876342

6. CUBLOIJ 8741023 6.____
LCLGCLB 1818914
JPUHIOC 3076158

7. OIJGCBPO 52398405 7.____
UHPBLIOP 76041250
CLUIPGPC 81720908

8. BPCOUOJI 40875732 8.____
UOHCIPLB 75682014
GLHUUCBJ 92677843

9. HOIOHJLH 65256361 9.____
IOJJHHBP 25536640
OJHBJOPI 53642502

Questions 10-13.

DIRECTIONS: Questions 10 through 13 are to be answered SOLELY on the basis of the information given in the following passage.

The mental attitude of the employee toward safety is exceedingly important in preventing accidents. All efforts designed to keep safety on the employee's mind and to keep accident prevention a live subject in the office will help substantially in a safety program. Although it may seem strange, it is common for people to be careless. Therefore, safety education is a continuous process.

Safety rules should be explained, and the reasons for their rigid enforcement should be given to employees. Telling employees to be careful or giving similar general safety warnings and slogans is probably of little value. Employees should be informed of basic safety fundamentals. This can be done through staff meetings, informal suggestions to employees, movies, and safety instruction cards. Safety instruction cards provide the employees with specific suggestions about safety and serve as a series of timely reminders helping to keep safety on the minds of employees. Pictures, posters, and cartoon sketches on bulletin boards that are located in areas continually used by employees arouse the employees' interest in safety. It is usually good to supplement this type of safety promotion with intensive individual follow-up.

10. The above passage implies that the LEAST effective of the following safety measures is 10.____

A. rigid enforcement of safety rules
B. getting employees to think in terms of safety
C. elimination of unsafe conditions in the office
D. telling employees to stay alert at all times

11. The reason given by the passage for maintaining ongoing safety education is that 11.____

A. people are often careless
B. office tasks are often dangerous
C. the value of safety slogans increases with repetition
D. safety rules change frequently

12. Which one of the following safety aids is MOST likely to be preferred by the passage? A 12.____

A. cartoon of a man tripping over a carton and yelling, *Keep aisles clear!*
B. poster with a large number one and a caption saying, *Safety First*
C. photograph of a very neatly arranged office
D. large sign with the word *THINK* in capital letters

13. Of the following, the BEST title for the above passage is 13.____

A. Basic Safety Fundamentals
B. Enforcing Safety Among Careless Employees
C. Attitudes Toward Safety
D. Making Employees Aware of Safety

Questions 14-21.

DIRECTIONS: Questions 14 through 21 are to be answered SOLELY on the basis of the information and the chart given below.

The following chart shows expenses in five selected categories for a one-year period, expressed as percentages of these same expenses during the previous year. The chart compares two different offices. In Office T (represented by), a cost reduction program has been tested for the past year. The other office, Office Q (represented by), served as a control, in that no special effort was made' to reduce costs during the past year.

RESULTS OF OFFICE COST REDUCTION PROGRAM

Expenses of Test and Control Groups for 2016
Expressed as Percentages of Same Expenses for 2015

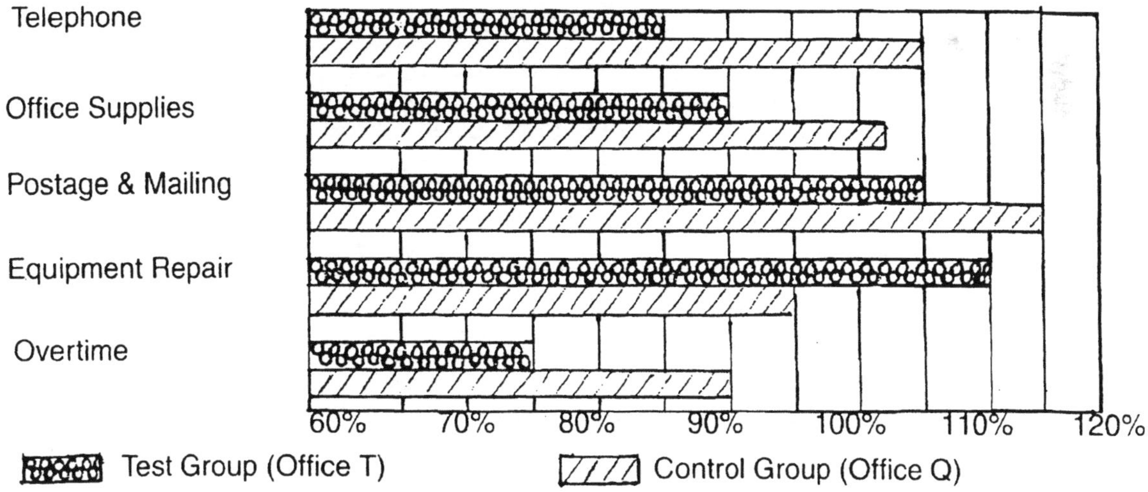

14. In Office T, which category of expense showed the greatest percentage REDUCTION from 2015 to 2016? 14.____

A. Telephone
B. Office Supplies
C. Postage & Mailing
D. Overtime

15. In which expense category did Office T show the BEST results in percentage terms when compared to Office Q? 15.____

A. Telephone
B. Office Supplies
C. Postage & Mailing
D. Overtime

16. According to the above chart, the cost reduction program was LEAST effective for the expense category of 16.____

A. Office Supplies
B. Postage & Mailing
C. Equipment Repair
D. Overtime

17. Office T's telephone costs went down during 2016 by approximately how many percentage points? 17.____

A. 15
B. 20
C. 85
D. 105

18. Which of the following changes occurred in expenses for Office Supplies in Office Q in the year 2016 as compared with the year 2015? 18.____
They

A. increased by more than 100%
B. remained the same
C. decreased by a few percentage points
D. increased by a few percentage points

19. For which of the following expense categories do the results in Office T and the results in Office Q differ MOST NEARLY by 10 percentage points? 19.____

A. Telephone
B. Postage & Mailing
C. Equipment Repair
D. Overtime

20. In which expense category did Office Q's costs show the GREATEST percentage increase in 2016? 20.____

A. Telephone
B. Office Supplies
C. Postage & Mailing
D. Equipment Repair

21. In Office T, by approximately what percentage did overtime expense change during the past year? 21.____
It

A. *increased* by 15%
B. *increased* by 75%
C. *decreased* by 10%
D. *decreased* by 25%

22. In a particular agency, there were 160 accidents in 2007. Of these accidents, 75% were due to unsafe acts and the rest were due to unsafe conditions. In the following year, a special safety program was established. The number of accidents in 2009 due to unsafe acts was reduced to 35% of what it had been in 2007. 22.____
How many accidents due to unsafe acts were there in 2009?

A. 20
B. 36
C. 42
D. 56

23. At the end of every month, the petty cash fund of Agency A is reimbursed for payments made from the fund during the month. During the month of February, the amounts paid from the fund were entered on receipts as follows: 10 bus fares of 35¢ each and one taxi fare of $3.50. 23.____
At the end of the month, the money left in the fund was in the following denominations: 15 one dollar bills, 4 quarters, 10 dimes, and 20 nickels.
If the petty cash fund is reduced by 20% for the following month, how much money will there be available in the petty cash fund for March?

A. $11.00
B. $20.00
C. $21.50
D. $25.00

24. The one of the following records which it would be MOST advisable to keep in alphabetical order is a 24.____

    A. continuous listing of phone messages, including time and caller, for your supervisor
    B. listing of individuals currently employed by your agency in a particular title
    C. record of purchases paid for by the petty cash fund
    D. dated record of employees who have borrowed material from the files in your office

25. Assume that you have been asked to copy by hand a column of numbers with two decimal places from one record to another. Each number consists of three, four, and five digits. 25.____
    In order to copy them quickly and accurately, you should copy

    A. each number exactly, making sure that the column of digits farthest to the right is in a straight line and all other columns are lined up
    B. the column of digits farthest to the right and then copy the next column of digits moving from right to left
    C. the column of digits farthest to the left and then copy the next column of digits moving from left to right
    D. the digits to the right of each decimal point and then copy the digits to the left of each decimal point

---

KEY (CORRECT ANSWERS)

1.	D	11.	A
2.	A	12.	A
3.	D	13.	D
4.	A	14.	D
5.	A	15.	A
6.	C	16.	C
7.	D	17.	A
8.	B	18.	D
9.	C	19.	B
10.	D	20.	C

21. D
22. C
23. B
24. B
25. A

EXAMINATION SECTION
TEST 1

DIRECTIONS: Each question or incomplete statement is followed by several suggested answers or completions. Select the one that BEST answers the question or completes the statement. *PRINT THE LETTER OF THE CORRECT ANSWER IN THE SPACE AT THE RIGHT.*

1. Assume that you are one of several clerks employed in the office of a city department. Members of the public occasionally visit the office to obtain information. Because your desk is nearest the entrance to the office, most of these visitors direct their inquiries to you. One morning when every one including yourself is busy, a visitor enters the office and asks you for some readily available information.
Of the following, the BEST action for you to take is to 1.______

   A. disregard his question in the hope that he will direct his inquiry to another clerk
   B. inform him politely that you are busy now and ask him to return in the afternoon
   C. give him the requested information concisely but courteously and then continue with your work
   D. advise him to write a letter to your department so that the information can be sent to him

2. As a clerk in the payroll bureau of a city department, you have been assigned the task of checking several payroll sheets. Your supervisor has informed you that these payroll sheets are needed by another department and must be sent to that department by 4 P.M. that day. After you have worked for a few hours, you realize that you will be unable to complete this assignment on time.
Of the following, the BEST action for you to take first is to 2.______

   A. ask a co-worker to help you
   B. check only those payroll sheets which you think are most important
   C. make sure that the payroll sheets which have been checked are sent out on time
   D. inform your supervisor of the situation

3. The switchboard operator of Department X refers a call to the department's Personnel Bureau. Miss Jones, a clerk in the Personnel Bureau, answers this call.
Of the following ways of answering this call, the MOST acceptable one is for Miss Jones to say 3.______

   A. "Hello."
   B. "Personnel Bureau, Miss Jones speaking."
   C. "Miss Jones speaking. To whom do you wish to speak?!'
   D. "Hello. This is Miss Jones of Department X."

4. A clerk in the mailing division of a large city department should be acquainted with the functions of the other divisions of the department CHIEFLY because he will be 4.______

   A. able to answer questions asked by visitors regarding the department
   B. more conscientious in doing his work if he knows that other divisions of the department perform important functions
   C. in a better position to make suggestions for improving the work of the various divisions of the department
   D. able to determine the proper division to which mail is to be forwarded

5. The central filing unit of a certain city department keeps in its files records used by the various bureaus in connection with their daily work. 5.______
It is desirable for the clerks in this filing unit to refile records as soon as possible after they have been returned by the different bureaus CHIEFLY because

A. records which are needed can be located most easily if they have been filed
B. such procedure develops commendable work habits among the employees
C. records which are not filed immediately are usually filed incorrectly
D. the accumulation of records to be filed gives the office a disorderly appearance

6. The active and inactive file material of an office is to be filed in several four-drawer filing cabinets. 6.______
Of the following, the BEST method of filing the material is, in general, to

A. keep inactive material in the upper drawers of the file cabinet so that such material may be easily removed for disposal
B. keep active material in the upper drawers so that the amount of stooping by clerks using the files is reduced to a minimum
C. assign drawers in the file cabinets alternately to active and to inactive material so that file material can be transferred easily from the active to the inactive files
D. assign file cabinets alternately to active and to inactive material so that cross-references between the two types of material can be easily made

7. Of the following, the BEST reason for using form letters is that they 7.______

A. enable an individual to transmit unpleasant or disappointing communications in a gentle and sympathetic manner
B. present the facts in a terse, business-like manner
C. save the time of both the dictator and the typist in answering letters dealing with similar matters
D. are flexible and can be easily changed to meet varying needs and complex situations

8. City agencies use either window envelopes or plain envelopes in mailing their correspondence, depending upon the type of mail being sent out. 8.____
When a mail clerk uses a window envelope rather than a plain envelope, he should be especially careful in

A. sealing and stamping the envelope
B. affixing the correct amount of postage
C. folding and inserting the communication
D. checking the return address

9. As a mail clerk, you have been instructed to make sure that an important letter is received by the person to whom it is addressed. 9.____

Of the following, the BEST action for you to take is to send the letter by

A. registered mail
B. special delivery
C. air mail
D. first-class mail

10. In filing, a clerk must often attach several papers together before placing them in the files. Usually, the MOST desirable of the following methods of attaching these papers is to 10.____

A. pin them together
B. staple them together
C. attach them with a paper clip
D. glue them together

11. It is a common practice in answering a letter of inquiry to make a copy of the reply. A clerk should know that, of the following, the BEST procedure to follow with the copy is to 11.____

A. file it with the letter it answers
B. file it alphabetically in a separate copy file
C. file it chronologically in a separate copy file and destroy the copy after thirty days
D. enclose it with the letter of reply

12. Suppose that much of the work of your office involves computation of statistical data. This computation is being done without the use of adding machines. You believe the work could be done more efficiently if adding machines were used.
Of the following, the BEST action for you to take is to 12.____

A. carry out your assignments without comment, since it is not your function to recommend revisions in office practices
B. have other clerks who agree with you sign a memorandum requesting your supervisor to install adding machines
C. obtain concrete facts to support your views and then take this matter up with your supervisor
D. point out to your supervisor every time an error is made that it would not have occurred if adding machines had been used

13. A clerk employed in the central file section of a city department has been requested to obtain a certain card which is kept in an alphabetic file containing several thousand cards. The clerk finds that this card is not in its proper place and that there is no out card to aid him in tracing its location.
Of the following, the course of action which would be LEAST helpful to him in locating the missing card would be for him to 13.____

A. secure the assistance of his superior
B. look at several cards filed immediately before and after the place where the missing card should be filed
C. ask the other clerks in the file section whether they have this card
D. prepare an out card and place it where the missing card should be filed

14. The one of the following types of computer software which requires the use of spreadsheets is 14.____

A. Excel
B. Acrobat
C. Outlook
D. Safari

15. A clerk assigned to file correspondence in a subject file would be MOST concerned with the 15.____

A. name of the sender
B. main topic of the correspondence
C. city and state of the sender
D. date of the correspondence

16. Assume that you are responsible for storing and distributing supplies in a city department. The one of the following factors which you should consider LEAST important in selecting a suitable place in the stock room for storing a particular item is 16.____

A. the frequency of requests for it
B. its perishability
C. its size
D. the importance of the bureaus using it

17. A clerk in charge of the supply room of a city department notices that one of the bureaus is asking for considerably more stationery than it has requested in the past. For him to inquire into the reasons for the increased demand would be 17.____

A. *desirable*; the amount of stationery used by a bureau should remain constant
B. *undesirable*; the increased demand may be due to waste, a condition beyond his control
C. *desirable*; he will be better able to estimate future needs for stationery
D. *undesirable*; he may be accused of meddling in matters which do not concern him

18. One of the first things an executive usually looks for when he arrives in the morning is his mail. Of the following, the MOST valid implication on the basis of this statement is that 18.____

A. letters addressed to an executive should be answered in the order in which they are received
B. whenever possible, mail for an executive should be on his desk before his arrival in the morning
C. letters to a city department should be addressed to the department head
D. the first task of an executive upon his arrival in the morning should be to answer his mail

19. Persons in the employ of a public agency generally come into contact with many people outside of working hours. In these contacts, the government employee represents to the public the quality, competence, and stature of public employees as a group. The one of the following statements which is the MOST valid implication of the above observation is that 19.____

A. the responsibilities of a public employee cease after office hours
B. government employees who come into contact with the public during working hours should be more efficient than those who have no contact with the public
C. a public employee, by his behavior during social activities, can raise the prestige of public employment
D. employees of a private company have greater responsibilities during office hours than employees of a public agency

20. Filing, in a way, is a form of recording. 20.____

The one of the following which BEST explains this statement is that
A. no other records are required if a proper filing system is used
B. important records should, as a rule, be kept in filing cabinets
C. a good system of record keeping eliminates the necessity for a filing system
D. filing a letter or document is, in effect, equivalent to making a record of its contents

21. In standardizing clerical tasks, one should attempt to eliminate the undesirable elements and to retain the desirable ones. 21.______
Of the following, the MOST valid implication of the above statement is that

A. a task containing undesirable elements cannot be standardized
B. standardized clerical tasks should not contain any unnecessary steps
C. interesting clerical tasks are easier to standardize than monotonous clerical tasks
D. a clerical task cannot have both desirable and undesirable elements

22. The efficiency of office workers in affected by the quality of the services provided to facilitate their work. 22.______
The one of the following statements which is the BEST illustration of the above judgment is that

A. a poorly run mail room will hamper the work of the office staff
B. continual tardiness on the part of an office worker will be reflected in the erformance of his work
C. a system of promoting office workers through competitive examinations will increase their efficiency
D. the use of a time clock will improve the quality of the work performed

23. In elections held in various states, the provisions relating to veterans' preference have been amended to conform with Federal practice. 23.______
In general, the MOST accurate statement regarding veterans' preference in civil service open competitive examinations for original appointment is that

A. disabled veterans passing an examination will be given 10 additional points and non-disabled veterans passing an examination will be given 5 additional points
B. disabled veterans passing an examination will be placed on top of the eligible list; non-disabled veterans will be placed after them; and non-veterans will be placed last on the list
C. only disabled veterans will be given 5 additional points; no additional points will be given to nondisabled veterans
D. the granting of additional points to all disabled and non-disabled veterans will be discontinued

24. Suppose that you are assigned to the information desk in your department. Your function is to give information to members of the public who telephone or call in person. It is a busy period of the year. There is a line of seventeen people waiting to speak to you. Because you are constantly being interrupted by telephone calls for information, however, you are unable to give any attention to the people waiting on line. The line is increasing in length. 24.______
Of the following, the BEST action for you to take is to

A. explain courteously to the people on line that you will probably be unable to help them
B. advise the people at the end of the line that you will probably not reach them for some time and suggest that they come back when you are less busy
C. ask the switchboard operator to answer telephone requests for information herself instead of putting the calls on your extension
D. ask your supervisor to assign another clerk to answer telephone calls so that you can give your full attention to the people on line

25. Suppose that you are acting as the receptionist in your department. A man comes up to you, introduces himself as Mr. Smith, and says that he has an appointment with Mr. Brown, one of the clerks in your department. You know that Mr. Brown has been called out of the office for a few days on important business. Upon learning of Mr. Brown's absence, Mr. Smith asks whether someone else can help him. For you to telephone Mr. Brown's office and ask whether some other clerk there can help Mr. Smith would be WISE mainly because 25._____

A. Mr. Smith's business is probably confidential
B. another clerk has probably been assigned to do Mr. Brown's work in Mr. Brown's absence
C. Mr. Brown may return unexpectedly
D. it is uncertain whether Mr. Smith actually does have an appointment with Mr. Brown

26. One of your duties may be to deliver copies of administrative orders to administrators in your department. It is not necessary for an administrator to sign a receipt for his copy of an order. One of the administrators to whom you are requested to deliver a copy of an order is not at his desk when you make your usual tour of the office. Of the following, the BEST action for you to take is to 26._____

A. keep this order until a later order is issued and then deliver both orders at the same time
B. wait until you meet the administrator in the corridor and give him his copy in person
C. leave a note on the administrator's desk requesting him to call
D. leave the administrator's copy of the order on his desk

27. One of your duties may be to deliver inter-office mail to all of the offices in the department in which you work.
Of the following, the BEST procedure for you to follow before you deliver the letters is, in general, to arrange them on the basis of the 27._____

A. offices to which the letters are to be delivered
B. dates on which the letters were written
C. specific persons by whom the letters were signed
D. offices from which the letters come

28. The population census of the country is undertaken every ten years by the United States Department of 28._____
A. Labor B. the Treasury C. Commerce D. the Interior

29. Of the following pairs of offices in the Federal government, the pair which is held by the same individual is 29._____
A. Secretary of Defense and Secretary of the Army
B. Chairman of the Atomic Energy Commission and Chairman of the Tennessee Valley Authority
C. Chief Justice of the United States Supreme Court and Attorney General
D. Vice President of the United States and President of the Senate

30. A clerk who is familiar with the organization and activities of the United Nations should know, of the following statements, the MOST accurate one is that 30._____
A. the permanent headquarters of the United Nations is in Geneva, Switzerland
B. devaluation of the currency of a member nation must be approved by the United Nations General Assembly
C. there are five permanent members on the United Nations Security Council
D. the Economic Cooperation Administration (ECA) is under the jurisdiction of the United Nations Secretary General

31. In anticipation of a seasonal increase in the amount of work to be performed by his division, a division chief prepared the following list of additional temporary employees needed by his division and the amount of time they would be employed: 31._____

26 cashiers, each at $24,000 a year, for 2 months
15 laborers, each at $85.00 a day, for 50 days
6 clerks, each at $21,000 a year, for 3 months

The total approximate cost for this additional personnel would be MOST NEARLY

A. $200,000　　B. $250,000　　C. $500,000　　D. $600,000

32. A calculating machine company offered to sell a city agency 4 calculating machines at a discount of 15% from the list price, and to allow the agency $85 for each of its two old machines. The list price of the new machines is $625 per machine. 32._____
If the city agency accepts this offer, the amount of money it will have to provide for the purchase of these four machines is

A. $1,785　　B. $2,295　　C. $1,955　　D. $1,836

33. A stationery buyer was offered bond paper at the following price scale: 33._____

$2.86 per ream for the first 1,000 reams
$2.60 per ream for the next 4,000 reams
$2.40 per ream for each additional ream beyond 5,000 reams

If the buyer ordered 10,000 reams of paper, the average cost per ream, computed to the NEAREST cent, was

A. $2.48　　B. $2.53　　C. $2.62　　D. $2.72

34. A clerk has 5.70% of his salary deducted for his retirement pension. 34._____
If this clerk's annual salary is $20,400, the monthly deduction for his retirement pension is

A. $298.20　　B. $357.90　　C. $1,162.80　　D. $96.90

35. In a certain bureau, two-thirds of the employees are clerks and the remainder is typists. 35._____
If there are 90 clerks, then the number of typists in this bureau is

A. 135　　B. 45　　C. 120　　D. 30

Questions 36-45.

DIRECTIONS: Assume that the code tables shown below are used by a city department in classifying its employees. Questions 36 to 45 are to be answered on the basis of these tables. In accordance with these code tables, each employee in the department is assigned a code number consisting of ten digits arranged from left to right in the following order:

I. Division in which Employed
II. Title of Position
III. Annual Salary
IV. Age
V. Number of Years Employed in Department

Example: A clerk is 21 years old, has been employed in the department for three years, and is working in the Supply Division at a yearly salary of $25,000. His code number should be 90-115-13-02-2.

Questions 36-45.

DIRECTIONS: Assume that the code tables shown below are used by a city department in classifying its employees. Questions 36 to 45 are to be answered on the basis of these tables. In accordance with these code tables, each employee in the department is assigned a code number consisting of ten digits arranged from left to right in the following order:

VI. Division in which Employed
VII. Title of Position
VIII. Annual Salary
IX. Age
X. Number of Years Employed in Department

Example: A clerk is 21 years old, has been employed in the department for three years, and is working in the Supply Division at a yearly salary of $25,000. His code number should be 90-115-13-02-2.

DEPARTMENTAL CODE

TABLE I		TABLE II		TABLE III		TABLE IV		TABLE V	
Code No.	Division in Which Employed	Code No.	Title of position	Code No.	Annual Salary	Code No.	Age	Code No.	No. of years Employed in Dept.
10-	Accounting Division	115-	Clek	11-	$18,000 or less	01-	under 20 yrs	1-	less than 1 yrs
20-	Construction Division	155-	Typist	12-	$18,001 to $24,000	02-	20 to 29 yrs	2-	1 to 5 yrs
30-	Engineering Division	175-	Steno-grapher	13-	$24,001 to $30,000	03-	30 to 39 yrs	3-	6 to 10 yrs
40-	Information Division	237-	Book-Keeper	14-	$30,001 to $36,000	04-	40 to 49 yrs	4-	11 to 15 yrs
50-	Maintenance Division	345-	Statis-tician	15-	$36,001 to $45,000	05-	50 to 59 yrs	5-	16 to 25 yrs
60-	Personnel Division	545-	Store-Keeper	16-	$45,001 to $60,000	06-	62 to 69 yrs	6-	26 to 35 yrs
70-	Record Division	633-	Drafts-Man	17-	$60,001 to $70,000	07- over	70 yrs or	7-	36 yrs. or over
80-	Research Division	665-	Civil-Engineer	18-	$70,001 or over				
90-	Supply Division	865-	Machinist						
		915-	Porter						

36. A draftsman employed in the Engineering Division yearly salary of $34,800 is 36 years old and has employed in the department for 9 years. 36.______
He should be coded

A. 20-633-13-04-3
B. 50-665-14-04-4
C. 30-865-13-03-4
D. 30-633-14-03-3

37. A porter employed in the Maintenance Division at a yearly salary of $28,800 is 52 years old and has been employed in the department for 6 years. 37.______
He should be coded

A. 50-915-12-03-3
B. 90-545-12-05-3
C. 50-915-13-05-3
D. 90-545-13-03-3

38. Richard White, who has been employed in the department for 12 years, receives $50,000 a year as a civil engineer in the Construction Division. He is 38 years old. 38.______
He should be coded

A. 20-665-16-03-4
B. 20-665-15-02-1
C. 20-633-14-04-2
D. 20-865-15-02-5

39. An 18-year-old clerk appointed to the department six months ago is assigned to the Record Division. His annual salary is $21,600. 39.______
He should be coded

A. 70-115-11-01-1
B. 70-115-12-01-1
C. 70-115-12-02-1
D. 70-155-12-01-1

40. An employee has been coded 40-155-12-03-3. 40.______
Of the following statements made regarding this employee, the MOST accurate one is that he is

A. a clerk who has been employed in the department for at least 6 years
B. a typist who receives an annual salary which does not exceed $24,000
C. under 30 years of age and has been employed in the department for at least 11 years
D. employed in the Supply Division at a salary which exceeds $18,000 per annum

41. Of the following statements regarding an employee who is coded 60-175-13-01-2, the LEAST accurate statement is that this employee 41.______

A. is a stenographer in the Personnel Division
B. has been employed in the department for at least one year
C. receives an annual salary which exceeds $24,000
D. is more than 20 years of age

42. The following are the names of our employees of the department with their code numbers: 42.______

James Black, 80-345-15-03-4;
William White, 30-633-14-03-4;
Sam Green, 80-115-12-02-3;
John Jones, 10-237-13-04-5.

If a salary increase is to be given to the employees who have been employed in the department for 11 years or more and who earn less than $36,001 a year, the two of the above employees who will receive a salary increase are

A. John Jones and William White
B. James Black and Sam Green
C. James Black and William White
D. John Jones and Sam Green

43. Code number 50-865-14-02-6, which has been assigned to a machinist, contains an obvious inconsistency. This inconsistency involves the figures 43.______

A. 50-865 B. 865-14 C. 14-02 D. 02-6

44. Ten employees were awarded merit prizes for outstanding service during the year. Their code numbers were: 44.______

80-345-14-04-4	40-155-12-02-2
40-155-12-04-4	10-115-12-02-2
10-115-13-03-2	80-115-13-02-2
80-175-13-05-5	10-115-13-02-3
10-115-12-04-3	30-633-14-04-4

Of these ten outstanding employees, the number who were clerks employed in the Accounting Division at a salary ranging from $24,001 to $30,000 per annum is

A. 1 B. 2 C. 3 D. 4

45. The MOST accurate of the following statements regarding the ten outstanding employees listed in Question 44 above is that 45.______

A. fewer than half of the employees were under 40 years of age
B. there were fewer typists than stenographers
C. four of the employees were employed in the department 11 years or more
D. two of the employees in the Research Division receive annual salaries ranging from $30,001 to $36,000

Questions 46-55.

DIRECTIONS: Questions 46 to 55 consist of groups of names. For each group, three different filing arrangements of the names in the group are given. In only one of these arrangements are the names in correct filing order according to the alphabetic filing rules which are given below. For each group, select the one arrangement, lettered A, B, or C, which is CORRECT and indicate in the space at the right the letter which corresponds to the CORRECT arrangement of names.

RULES FOR ALPHABETIC FILING

NAMES OF INDIVIDUALS

(1) The names of individuals are to be filed in strict alphabetic order. The order of filing is: first according to the last name; then according to the first name or initial; and finally according to the middle name or initial.

(2) Where two last names are identical, the one with an initial instead of the first name precedes the one with a first name beginning with the same initial letter. For example: D. Smith and D.J. Smith precede Donald Smith.

(3) Where two individuals with identical last names also have identical first names or initials, the one without a middle name or initial precedes the one with a middle name or initial. For example: D. Smith precedes D.J. Smith, and Donald Smith precedes Donald J. Smith.

(4) Where two individuals with identical last names also have identical first names or initials, the one with an initial instead of the middle name precedes the one with a middle name beginning with the same initial letter. For example: Donald J. Smith precedes Donald Joseph Smith.

NAMES OF BUSINESS ORGANIZATIONS

The names of business organizations are to be filed in alphabetic order as written, except that the names of an organization containing the name of an individual is filed alphabetically according to the name of the individual as described in the above rules. For example: John Burke Wine Co. precedes Central Storage Corp.

ADDITIONAL RULES

(1) Names composed of numerals or of abbreviations of names are to be treated as if the numerals or the abbreviations were spelled out.
(2) Prefixes such as De, Di, O', Le, and La are considered as part of the names they precede.
(3) Names beginning with "Mc" and "Mac" are to be filed as spelled.
(4) The following titles and designations are to be disregarded in filing: Dr., Mr., Jr., Sr., D.D.S., and M.D.
(5) The following are to be disregarded when they occur in the names of business organizations: the, of, and.

SAMPLE ITEM:

ARRANGEMENT A	ARRANGEMENT B	ARRANGEMENT C
Robert Morse	R. Moss	R. T. Morse
Ralph Nixon	R. T. Morse	Robert Morse
R. T. Morse	Ralph Nixon	R. Moss
R. Moss	Robert Morse	Ralph Nixon

The CORRECT arrangement is C; the answer should, therefore, be C

46.

ARRANGMENT A	ARRANGEMENT B	ARRANGEMENT C
R. B. Stevens	Aled T. Stevens	R.Stevens
Chas. Stevennson	R. B. Stevens	Robert Stevens, Sr.
Robert Stevensm, Sr.	Robert Stevens, Sr.	Alfred T. Steven s
Alfred T. Stevens	Chas. Stevenson	Chas. Stevenson

46._____

47.

ARRANGEMENT A	ARRANGEMENT B	ARRANGEMENT C
Mr. A. T. Breen	John Brewington	Dr. Otis C. Breen
Dr. Otis C. Breen	Amelia K. Brewington	Mr. A. T. Breen
Amelia K Brewington	Dr. Otis C. Breen	John Brewington
John Brewington	Mr. A. T. Breen	Amelia K. Brewington

47._____

48. ARRANGEMENT A
J. Murphy
J. J. Murphy
John Murphy
John J. Murphy

ARRANGEMENT B
John Murphy
John J. Murphy
J. Murphy
J. J. Murphy

ARRANGEMENT C
J. Murphy
John Murphy
J. J. Murphy
John J. Murphy

48._____

49. ARRANGEMENT A
Anthoney Dibuono
George Burns, Sr
Geo. T. Burns, Jr.
Alan J. Byrnes

ARRANGEMENT B
Geo. T. Burns, Jr.
George Burns, Sr.
Anthony DiBuono
Alan J. Byrnes

ARRANGEMENT C
George Burns, Sr.
George T. Burns, Jr.
Alan J. Byrnes
Anthony DiBuono

49._____

50. ARRANGEMENT A
James Macauley
Frank A. Mclowery
Francis Maclaughry
Bernard J. MacMahon

ARRANGEMENT B
James Macauley
Francis Macloughry
Bernard J.Macmahon
Frank A. McLowery

ARRANGEMENT C
Bernard J. Macmahon
Francis MacLaughry
Frank A. McLowery
James Macauley

50._____

51. ARRANGEMENT A
A. J. DiBartolo, Sr.
A. P.DiBartolo
J. A. Bartolo
Anthony J. Bartolo

ARRANGEMENT B
J. A. Bartolo
Anthony J. Bartolo
A. J. DiBartolo
A. J. DiBartolo, Sr.

ARRANGEMENT C
Anthony J. Bartolo
J. A. Bartolo
A. J. DiBartolo, Sr
A. P. DiBartolo

51._____

52. ARRANGEMENT A
Edward Holmes Corp.
Hillside Trust Corp.
Standard Insurance Co.
The Industrial Surety Co

ARRANGEMENT B
Edward Holmes Corp.
Hillside Trust Corp.
The Industrial Surety Co.
Standard Insurance Co.

ARRANGEMENT C
Hillside Trust Corp.
Edward Holmes Corp
The Industrial Surety Co.
Standard Insurance Co.

52._____

53. ARRANGEMENT A
Cooperative Credit Co.
Chas. Cooke Chemical Corp.
John Fuller Baking Co.
4th Avenue Express Co.

ARRANGEMENT B
Chas, Cooke Chemical Corp.
Cooperative Credit Co.
4th Avenue Express Co.
John Fuller Baking Co.

53._____

ARRANGEMENT C
4th Avenue Express Co.
John Fuller Baking Co.
Chas. Cooke Chemical Corp.
Cooperative Credit Co.

54. ARRANGEMENT A
Mr. R. McDaniels
Robert Darling, Jr.
F. L. Ramsey
Charles DeRhone

ARRANGEMENT B
F. L. Ramsey
Mr. R. McDaniels
Charles DeRhone
Robert Darling, Jr.

ARRANGEMENT C
Robert darling, Jr.
Charles DeRhone
Mr. R. Mcdaniels
F. L. Ramsey

54._____

55.

ARRANGEMENT A	ARRANGEMENT B	ARRANGEMENT C
New York Ominibus Corp.	John J. O'Brien Co.	Nova Scotia Canning Co.
New York Shipping Co.	New York Ominibus Ciorp.	John J. O'Brien Co.
Nove Scotia Canning Co.	New York Shipping Co.	New York Ominibus Corp.
John J. O'Brien Co.	Nove Scotia Canning Co.	New York shipping Co.

55._____

56. He was asked to *pacify* the visitor. The word pacify means MOST NEARLY 56._____

A. escort B. interview C. calm D. detain

57. To say that a certain document is *authentic* means MOST NEARLY that it is 57._____

A. fictitious B. well written C. priceless D. genuine

58. A clerk who is *meticulous* in performing his work is one who is 58._____

A. alert to improved techniques
B. likely to be erratic and unpredictable
C. excessively careful of small details
D. slovenly and inaccurate

59 A pamphlet which is *replete* with charts and graphs is one which 59._____

A. deals with the construction of charts and graphs
B. is full of charts and graphs
C. substitutes illustrations for tabulated data
D. is in need of charts and graphs

60. His former secretary was *diligent* in carrying out her duties. The word diligent means MOST NEARLY 60._____

A. incompetent B. cheerful C. careless D. industrious

61. To supepsede means MOST NEARLY to 61._____

A. take the place of B. come before
C. be in charge of D. divide into equal parts

62. He sent the *irate* employee to the pepsonnel manager. The word *irate* means MOST NEARLY 62._____

A. irresponsible B. untidy C. insubordinate D. angry

63. An *ambiguous* statement is one which is 63._____
A forceful and convincing
B capable of being understood in more than one sense
C based upon good judgment and sound reasoning processes
D uninteresting and too lengthy

64. To *extol* means MOST NEARLY to 64.____

A. summon B. praise C. reject D. withdraw

65. The word *proximity* means MOST NEARLY 65.____

A. similarity B. exactness C. harmony D. nearness

66. His friends had a *detrimental* influence on him. The word detrimental means MOST NEARLY 66.____

A. favorable B. lasting C. harmful D. short-lived

67. The chief inspector relied upon the *veracity* of his inspectors. The word veracity means MOST NEARLY 67.____

A. speed B. assistance C. shrewdness D. truthfulness

68. There was much *diversity* in the suggestions submitted. The word diversity means MOST NEARLY 68.____

A. similarity B. value C. triviality D. variety

69. The survey was concerned with the problem of *indigence.* The word indigence means MOST NEARLY 69.____

A. poverty B. corruption C. intolerance D. morale

70. The investigator considered this evidence to be *extraneous.* The word extraneous means MOST NEARLY 70.____

A. significant
B. pertinent but unobtainable
C. not essential
D. inadequate

71. He was surppised at the *temerity* of the new employee. The word temerity means MOST NEARLY 71.____

A. shyness B. enthusiasm C. rashness D. self-control

72. The term *ex officio* means MOST NEARLY 72.____

A. expelled from office
B. a former holder of a high office
C. without official approval
D. by virtue of office or position

Questions 73-82.

DIRECTIONS: Questions 73 to 82 consist of four words each. One word in each row is INCORRECTLY spelled. For each item, print in the correspondingly numbered space at the right the letter preceding the word which is INCORRECTLY spelled.

73. A. apparent B. superintendent C. releive D. calendar 73.____

74. A. foreign B. negotiate C. typical D. discipline 74.____

75. A. posponed B. argument C. susceptible D. deficit 75.____

76. A. preferred B. column C. peculiar D. equiped 76.____

77.	A.	exaggerate	B.	disatisfied	C.	repetition	D.	already	77.____
78.	A.	livelihood	B.	physician	C.	obsticle	D.	strategy	78.____
79.	A.	courageous	B.	ommission	C.	ridiculous	D.	awkward	79.____
80.	A.	sincerely	B.	abundance	C.	negligable	D.	elementary	80.____
81.	A.	obsolete	B.	mischievous	C.	enumerate	D.	atheletic	81.____
82.	A.	fiscel	B.	beneficiary	C.	concede	D.	translate	82.____

Questions 83-97

DIRECTIONS: Each of the following sentences may be classified MOST appropriately under one of the following four categories:

A. faulty because of incorrect grammar
B. faulty because of incorrect punctuation
C. faulty because of incorrect capitalization
D. correct

Examine each sentence carefully. Then, in the correspondingly numbered space at the right, print the letter preceding the option which is the BEST of the four suggested above. All incorrect sentences contain but one type of error. Consider a sentence correct if it contains none of the types of errors mentioned, even though there may be other eorrect ways of expressing the same thought.

83. Neither of the two administrators are going to attend the conference being held in Washington, D.C. 83.____

84. Since Miss Smith and Miss Jones have more experience than us, they have been given more responsible duties. 84.____

85. Mr. Shaw the supervisor of the stock room maintains an inventory of stationery and office supplies. 85.____

86. Inasmuch as this matter affects both you and I, we should take joint action. 86.____

87. Who do you think will be able to perform this highly technical work? 87.____

88. Of the two employees, John is considered the most competent. 88.____

89. He is not coming home on tuesday; we expect him next week. 89.____

90. Stenographers, as well as typists must be able to type rapidly and accurately. 90.____

91. Having been placed in the safe we were sure that the money would not be stolen 91.____

92. Only the employees who worked overtime last week may leave one hour earlier today. 92.____

93. We need someone who can speak french fluently. 93.____

94. A tall, elderly, man entered the office and asked to see Mr. Brown. 94.____

95. The clerk insisted that he had filed the correspondence in the proper cabinet. 95.____

96. "Will you assist us," he asked? 96.____

97. According to the information contained in the report, a large quantity of paper and envelopes were used by this bureau last year. 97.____

Questions 98-100.

DIRECTIONS: Items 98 to 100 are a test of your proofreading ability.
Each item consists of Copy I and Copy II. You are to assume that Copy I in each item is correct. Copy II, which is meant to be a duplicate of Copy I, may contain some typographical errors.. In each item, compare Copy II with Copy I and determine the number of errors in Copy II. If there are:
no errors, mark your answer A;
1 or 2 errors, mark your answer B;
3 or 4 errors, mark your answer C;
5 or 6 errors, mark your answer D;
7 errors or more, mark your answer E.

98. COPY I 98.____
The Commissioner, before issuing any such license, shall cause an investigation to be made of the premises named and described in such application, to determine whether all the provisions of the sanitary code, building code, state industrial code, state minimum wage law, local laws, regulations of municipal agencies, and other requirements of this article are fully observed. (Section B32-169.0 of Article 23.)

COPY II
The Commissioner, before issuing any such license shall cause an investigation to be made of the premises named and described tn such applecation, to determine whether all the provisions of the sanitary code, bilding code, state tndustrial code, state minimum wage laws, local laws, regulations of municipal agencies, and other requirements of this article are fully observed. (Section E32-169.0 of Article 23.)

99. COPY I 99.____
Among the persons who have been appointed to various agencies are John Queen, 9 West 55th Street, Brooklyn; Joseph Blount, 2497 Durward Road, Bronx; Lawrence K. Eberhardt, 3194 Bedford Street, Manhattan; Reginald L. Darcy, 1476 Allerton Drive, Bronx; and Benjamin Ledwith, 177 Greene Street, Manhattan.

COPY II
Among the persons who have been appointed to various agencies are John Queen, 9 West 56th Street,Brooklyn, Joseph Blount, 2497 Dureward Road, Bronx; Lawrence K. Eberhart, 3194 Belford Street, Manhattan; Reginald L. Darcey, 1476 Allerton drive, Bronx; and Benjamin Ledwith, 177 Green Street, Manhattan.

100. COPY I 100.____
Except as hereinafter provided, it shall be unlawful to use, store or have on hand any inflammable motion picture film in quantities greater than one standard or two sub-standard reels, or aggregating more than two thousand feet in length, or more than ten pounds in weight without the permit required by this section.

COPY II
Except as herinafter provided, it shall be unlawfull to use, store or have on hand any inflammable motion picture film, in quantities greater than one standard or two substandard reels or aggregating more than two thousand feet in length, or more than ten pounds in weight without the permit required by this section.

17

KEY (CORRECT ANSWERS)

1. C
2. D
3. B
4. D
5. A
6. B
7. C
8. C
9. A
10. B
11. A
12. C
13. D
14. A
15. B
16. D
17. C
18. B
19. C
20. D
21. B
22. A
23. A
24. D
25. B
26. D
27. A
28. C
29. D
30. C
31. A
32. C
33. B
34. D
35. B
36. B
37. C
38. A
39. B
40. B
41. D
42. A
43. D
44. B
45. C
46. B
47. A
48. A
49. C
50. B
51. C
52. C
53. B
54. C
55. A
56. C
57. D
58. C
59. B
60. D
61. A
62. D
63. B
64. B
65. D
66. C
67. D
68. D
69. A
70. C
71. C
72. D
73. C
74. D
75. A
76. D
77. B
78. C
79. B
80. C
81. D
82. A
83. A
84. A
85. B
86. A
87. D
88. A
89. C
90. B
91. A
92. D
93. C
94. B
95. D
96. B
97. A
98. D
99. E
100. E

READING COMPREHENSION
UNDERSTANDING AND INTERPRETING WRITTEN MATERIAL
EXAMINATION SECTION
TEST 1

DIRECTIONS: Each question or incomplete statement is followed by several suggested answers or completions. Select the one that BEST answers the question or completes the statement. *PRINT THE LETTER OF THE CORRECT ANSWER IN THE SPACE AT THE RIGHT.*

Questions 1-3.

DIRECTIONS: Questions 1 through 3 are to be answered SOLELY on the basis of the following statement.

The equipment in a mailroom may include a mail metering machine. This machine simultaneously stamps, postmarks, seals, and counts letters as fast as the operator can feed them. It can also print the proper postage directly on a gummed strip to be affixed to bulky items. It is equipped with a meter which is removed from the machine and sent to the postmaster to be set for a given number of stampings of any denomination. The setting of the meter must be paid for in advance. One of the advantages of metered mail is that it bypasses the cancellation operation and thereby facilitates handling by the post office. Mail metering also makes the pilfering of stamps impossible, but does not prevent the passage of personal mail in company envelopes through the meters unless there is established a rigid control or censorship over outgoing mail.

1. According to this statement, the postmaster 1.____

   A. is responsible for training new clerks in the use of mail metering machines
   B. usually recommends that both large and small firms adopt the use of mail metering machines
   C. is responsible for setting the meter to print a fixed number of stampings
   D. examines the mail metering machine to see that they are properly installed in the mailroom

2. According to this statement, the use of mail metering machines 2.____

   A. requires the employment of more clerks in a mailroom than does the use of postage stamps
   B. interferes with the handling of large quantities of outgoing mail
   C. does not prevent employees from sending their personal letters at company expense
   D. usually involves smaller expenditures for mailroom equipment than does the use of postage stamps

3. On the basis of this statement, it is MOST accurate to state that 3.____

   A. mail metering machines are often used for opening envelopes
   B. postage stamps are generally used when bulky packages are to be mailed
   C. the use of metered mail tends to interfere with rapid mail handling by the post office
   D. mail metering machines can seal and count letters at the same time

Questions 4-5.

DIRECTIONS: Questions 4 and 5 are to be answered SOLELY on the basis of the following statement.

Forms are printed sheets of paper on which information is to be entered. While what is printed on the form is most important, the kind of paper used in making the form is also important. The kind of paper should be selected with regard to the use to which the form will be subjected. Printing a form on an unnecessarily expensive grade of papers is wasteful. On the other hand, using too cheap or flimsy a form can materially interfere with satisfactory performance of the work the form is being planned to do. Thus, a form printed on both sides normally requires a heavier paper than a form printed only on one side. Forms to be used as permanent records, or which are expected to have a very long life in files, requires a quality of paper which will not disintegrate or discolor with age. A form which will go through a great deal of handling requires a strong, tough paper, while thinness is a necessary qualification where the making of several copies of a form will be required.

4. According to this statement, the type of paper used for making forms 4.____

A. should be chosen in accordance with the use to which the form will be put
B. should be chosen before the type of printing to be used has been decided upon
C. is as important as the information which is printed on it
D. should be strong enough to be used for any purpose

5. According to this statement, forms that are 5.____

A. printed on both sides are usually economical and desirable
B. to be filed permanently should not deteriorate as time goes on
C. expected to last for a long time should be handled carefully
D. to be filed should not be printed on inexpensive paper

Questions 6-8.

DIRECTIONS: Questions 6 through 8 are to be answered SOLELY on the basis of the following paragraph.

The increase in the number of public documents in the last two centuries closely matches the increase in population in the United States. The great number of public documents has become a serious threat to their usefulness. It is necessary to have programs which will reduce the number of public documents that are kept and which will, at the same time, assure keeping those that have value. Such programs need a great deal of thought to have any success.

6. According to the above paragraph, public documents may be LESS useful if 6.____

A. the files are open to the public
B. the record room is too small
C. the copying machine is operated only during normal working hours
D. too many records are being kept

7. According to the above paragraph, the growth of the population in the United States has matched the growth in the quantity of public documents for a period of MOST NEARLY _______ years. 7._____

A. 50 B. 100 C. 200 D. 300

8. According to the above paragraph, the increased number of public documents has made it necessary to 8._____

A. find out which public documents are worth keeping
B. reduce the great number of public documents by decreasing government services
C. eliminate the copying of all original public documents
D. avoid all new copying devices

Questions 9-10.

DIRECTIONS: Questions 9 and 10 are to be answered SOLELY on the basis of the following paragraph.

The work goals of an agency can best be reached if the employees understand and agree with these goals. One way to gain such understanding and agreement is for management to encourage and seriously consider suggestions from employees in the setting of agency goals.

9. On the basis of the above paragraph, the BEST way to achieve the work goals of an agency is to 9._____

A. make certain that employees work as hard as possible
B. study the organizational structure of the agency
C. encourage employees to think seriously about the agency's problems
D. stimulate employee understanding of the work goals

10. On the basis of the above paragraph, understanding and agreement with agency goals can be gained by 10._____

A. allowing the employees to set agency goals
B. reaching agency goals quickly
C. legislative review of agency operations
D. employee participation in setting agency goals

Questions 11-13.

DIRECTIONS: Questions 11 through 13 are to be answered SOLELY on the basis of the following paragraph.

In order to organize records properly, it is necessary to start from their very beginning and trace each copy of the record to find out how it is used, how long it is used, and what may finally be done with it. Although several copies of the record are made, one copy should be marked as the copy of record. This is the formal legal copy, held to meet the requirements of the law. The other copies may be retained for brief periods for reference purposes, but these copies should not be kept after their usefulness as reference ends. There is another reason for tracing records through the office and that is to determine how long it takes the copy of record to reach the central file. The copy of record must not be kept longer than necessary by the section of the office which has prepared it, but should be sent to the central file as soon as possible so that it can be available to the various sections of the office. The central file can make the copy of record available to the various sections of the office at an early date only if it arrives at the central file as quickly as possible. Just as soon as its immediate or active service period is ended, the copy of record should be removed from the central file and put into the inactive file in the office to be stored for whatever length of time may be necessary to meet legal requirements, and then destroyed.

11. According to the above paragraph, a reason for tracing records through an office is to 11.____

A. determine how long the central file must keep the records
B. organize records properly
C. find out how many copies of each record are required
D. identify the copy of record

12. According to the above paragraph, in order for the central file to have the copy of record available as soon as possible for the various sections of the office, it is MOST important that the 12.____

A. copy of record to be sent to the central file meets the requirements of the law
B. copy of record is not kept in the inactive file too long
C. section preparing the copy of record does not unduly delay in sending it to the central file
D. central file does not keep the copy of record beyond its active service period

13. According to the above paragraph, the length of time a copy of a record is kept in the inactive file of an office depends CHIEFLY on the 13.____

A. requirements of the law
B. length of time that is required to trace the copy of record through the office
C. use that is made of the copy of record
D. length of the period that the copy of record is used for reference purposes

Questions 14-16.

DIRECTIONS: Questions 14 through 16 are to be answered SOLELY on the basis of the following paragraph.

The office was once considered as nothing more than a focal point of internal and external correspondence. It was capable only of dispatching a few letters upon occasion and of preparing records of little practical value. Under such a concept, the vitality of the office force was impaired. Initiative became stagnant, and the lot of the office worker was not likely to be a happy one. However, under the new concept of office management, the possibilities of waste and mismanagement in office operation are now fully recognized, as are the possibilities for the modern office to assist in the direction and control of business operations. Fortunately, the modern concept of the office as a centralized service-rendering unit is gaining ever greater acceptance in today's complex business world, for without the modern office, the production wheels do not turn and the distribution of goods and services is not possible.

14. According to the above paragraph, the fundamental difference between the old and the new concept of the office is the change in the 14.____

    A. accepted functions of the office
    B. content and the value of the records kept
    C. office methods and systems
    D. vitality and morale of the office force

15. According to the above paragraph, an office operated today under the old concept of the office MOST likely would 15.____

    A. make older workers happy in their jobs
    B. be part of an old thriving business concern
    C. have a passive role in the conduct of a business enterprise
    D. attract workers who do not believe in modern methods

16. Of the following, the MOST important implication of the above paragraph is that a present-day business organization cannot function effectively without the 16.____

    A. use of modern office equipment
    B. participation and cooperation of the office
    C. continued modernization of office procedures
    D. employment of office workers with skill and initiative

Questions 17-20.

DIRECTIONS: Questions 17 through 20 are to be answered SOLELY on the basis of the following paragraph.

A report is frequently ineffective because the person writing it is not fully acquainted with all the necessary details before he actually starts to construct the report. All details pertaining to the subject should be known before the report is started. If the essential facts are not known, they should be investigated. It is wise to have essential facts written down rather than to depend too much on memory, especially if the facts pertain to such matters as amounts, dates, names of persons, or other specific data. When the necessary information has been gathered, the general plan and content of the report should be thought out before the writing is actually begun. A person with little or no experience in writing reports may find that it is wise to make a brief outline. Persons with more experience should not need a written outline, but they should make mental notes of the steps they are to follow. If writing reports without dictation is a regular part of an office worker's duties, he should set aside a certain time during the day when he is least likely to be interrupted. That may be difficult, but in most offices there are certain times in the day when the callers, telephone calls, and other interruptions are not numerous. During those times, it is best to write reports that need undivided concentration. Reports that are written amid a series of interruptions may be poorly done.

17. Before starting to write an effective report, it is necessary to 17.____

    A. memorize all specific information
    B. disregard ambiguous data
    C. know all pertinent information
    D. develop a general plan

18. Reports dealing with complex and difficult material should be 18.____

A. prepared and written by the supervisor of the unit
B. written when there is the least chance of interruption
C. prepared and written as part of regular office routine
D. outlined and then dictated

19. According to the paragraph, employees with no prior familiarity in writing reports may find it helpful to 19.____

A. prepare a brief outline
B. mentally prepare a synopsis of the report's content
C. have a fellow employee help in writing the report
D. consult previous reports

20. In writing a report, needed information which is unclear should be 20.____

A. disregarded
B. memorized
C. investigated
D. gathered

Questions 21-25.

DIRECTIONS: Questions 21 through 25 are to be answered SOLELY on the basis of the following passage.

Positive discipline minimizes the amount of personal supervision required and aids in the maintenance of standards. When a new employee has been properly introduced and carefully instructed, when he has come to know the supervisor and has confidence in the supervisor's ability to take care of him, when he willingly cooperates with the supervisor, that employee has been under positive discipline and can be put on his own to produce the quantity and quality of work desired. Negative discipline, the fear of transfer to a less desirable location, for example, to a limited extent may restrain certain individuals from overt violation of rules and regulations governing attendance and conduct which in governmental agencies are usually on at least an agency-wide basis. Negative discipline may prompt employees to perform according to certain rules to avoid a penalty such as, for example, docking for tardiness.

21. According to the above passage, it is reasonable to assume that in the area of discipline, the first-line supervisor in a governmental agency has GREATER scope for action in 21.____

A. *positive* discipline, because negative discipline is largely taken care of by agency rules and regulations
B. *negative* discipline, because rules and procedures are already fixed and the supervisor can rely on them
C. *positive* discipline, because the supervisor is in a position to recommend transfers
D. *negative* discipline, because positive discipline is reserved for people on a higher supervisory level

22. In order to maintain positive discipline of employees under his supervision, it is MOST important for a supervisor to 22.____

A. assure each employee that he has nothing to worry about
B. insist at the outset on complete cooperation from employees

C. be sure that each employee is well trained in his job
D. inform new employees of the penalties for not meeting standards

23. According to the above passage, a feature of negative discipline is that it 23.____

A. may lower employee morale
B. may restrain employees from disobeying the rules
C. censures equal treatment of employees
D. tends to create standards for quality of work

24. A REASONABLE conclusion based on the above passage is that positive discipline benefits a supervisor because 24.____

A. he can turn over orientation and supervision of a new employee to one of his subordinates
B. subordinates learn to cooperate with one another when working on an assignment
C. it is easier to administer
D. it cuts down, in the long run, on the amount of time the supervisor needs to spend on direct supervision

25. Based on the above passage, it is REASONABLE to assume, that an important difference between positive discipline and negative discipline is that positive discipline 25.____

A. is concerned with the quality of work and negative discipline with the quantity of work
B. leads to a more desirable basis for motivation of the employee
C. is more likely to be concerned with agency rules and regulations
D. uses fear while negative discipline uses penalties to prod employees to adequate performance

---

KEY (CORRECT ANSWERS)

1.	C	11.	B
2.	C	12.	C
3.	D	13.	A
4.	A	14.	A
5.	B	15.	C
6.	D	16.	B
7.	C	17.	C
8.	A	18.	B
9.	D	19.	A
10.	D	20.	B

21. A
22. C
23. B
24. D
25. B

TEST 2

Questions 1-6.

DIRECTIONS: Questions 1 through 6 are to be answered SOLELY on the basis of the following passage.

Inherent in all organized endeavors is the need to resolve the individual differences involved in conflict. Conflict may be either a positive or negative factor since it may lead to creativity, innovation and progress on the one hand, or it may result, on the other hand, in a deterioration or even destruction of the organization. Thus, some forms of conflict are desirable, whereas others are undesirable and ethically wrong.

There are three management strategies which deal with interpersonal conflict. In the *divide-and-rule strategy,* management attempts to maintain control by limiting the conflict to those directly involved and preventing their disagreement from spreading to the larger group. The *suppression-of-differences strategy* entails ignoring conflicts or pretending they are irrelevant. In the *working-through-differences strategy,* management actively attempts to solve or resolve intergroup or interpersonal conflicts. Of the three strategies, only the last directly attacks and has the potential for eliminating the causes of conflict. An essential part of this strategy, however, is its employment by a committed and relatively mature management team.

1. According to the above passage, the *divide-and-rule strategy tor* dealing with conflict is the attempt to 1.____

   A. involve other people in the conflict
   B. restrict the conflict to those participating in it
   C. divide the conflict into positive and negative factors
   D. divide the conflict into a number of smaller ones

2. The word *conflict* is used in relation to both positive and negative factors in this passage. Which one of the following words is MOST likely to describe the activity which the word *conflict,* in the sense of the passage, implies? 2.____

   A. Competition B. Confusion
   C. Cooperation D. Aggression

3. According to the above passage, which one of the following characteristics is shared by both the *suppression-of-differences strategy* and the *divide-and-rule strategy?* 3.____

   A. Pretending that conflicts are irrelevant
   B. Preventing conflicts from spreading to the group situation
   C. Failure to directly attack the causes of conflict
   D. Actively attempting to resolve interpersonal conflict

4. According to the above passage, the successful resolution of interpersonal conflict requires 4.____

   A. allowing the group to mediate conflicts between two individuals
   B. division of the conflict into positive and negative factors
   C. involvement of a committed, mature management team
   D. ignoring minor conflicts until they threaten the organization

5. Which can be MOST reasonably inferred from the above passage? Conflict between two individuals is LEAST likely to continue when management uses 5.____

   A. the *working-through differences strategy*
   B. the *suppression-of differences strategy*
   C. the *divide-and-rule strategy*
   D. a combination of all three strategies

6. According to the above passage, a DESIRABLE result of conflict in an organization is when conflict 6.____

   A. exposes production problems in the organization
   B. can be easily ignored by management
   C. results in advancement of more efficient managers
   D. leads to development of new methods

Questions 7-13.

DIRECTIONS: Questions 7 through 13 are to be answered SOLELY on the basis of the passage below.

Modern management places great emphasis on the concept of communication. The communication process consists of the steps through which an idea or concept passes from its inception by one person, the sender, until it is acted upon by another person, the receiver. Through an understanding of these steps and some of the possible barriers that may occur, more effective communication may be achieved. The first step in the communication process is ideation by the sender. This is the formation of the intended content of the message he wants to transmit. In the next step, encoding, the sender organizes his ideas into a series of symbols designed to communicate his message to his intended receiver. He selects suitable words or phrases that can be understood by the receiver, and he also selects the appropriate media to be used—for example, memorandum, conference, etc. The third step is transmission of the encoded message through selected channels in the organizational structure. In the fourth step, the receiver enters the process by tuning in to receive the message. If the receiver does not function, however, the message is lost. For example, if the message is oral, the receiver must be a good listener. The fifth step is decoding of the message by the receiver, as for example, by changing words into ideas. At this step, the decoded message may not be the same idea that the sender originally encoded because the sender and receiver have different perceptions regarding the meaning of certain words. Finally, the receiver acts or responds. He may file the information, ask for more information, or take other action. There can be no assurance, however, that communication has taken place unless there is some type of feedback to the sender in the form of an acknowledgement that the message was received.

7. According to the above passage, *ideation* is the process by which the 7.____

   A. sender develops the intended content of the message
   B. sender organizes his ideas into a series of symbols
   C. receiver tunes in to receive the message
   D. receiver decodes the message

8. In the last sentence of the passage, the word *feedback* refers to the process by which the sender is assured that the 8.____

   A. receiver filed the information
   B. receiver's perception is the same as his own
   C. message was received
   D. message was properly interpreted

9. Which one of the following BEST shows the order of the steps in the communication process as described in the passage? 9.____

   A. 1 - ideation 2 - encoding
   3 - decoding 4 - transmission
   5 - receiving 6 - action
   7 - feedback to the sender

   B. 1 - ideation 2 - encoding
   3 - transmission 4 - decoding
   5 - receiving 6 - action
   7 - feedback to the sender

   C. 1 - ideation 2 - decoding
   3 - transmission 4 - receiving
   5 - encoding 6 - action
   7 - feedback to the sender

   D. 1 - ideation 2 - encoding
   3 - transmission 4 - receiving
   5 - decoding 6 - action
   7 - feedback to the sender

10. Which one of the following BEST expresses the main theme of the passage? 10.____

    A. Different individuals have the same perceptions regarding the meaning of words.
    B. An understanding of the steps in the communication process may achieve better communication.
    C. Receivers play a passive role in the communication process.
    D. Senders should not communicate with receivers who transmit feedback.

11. The above passage implies that a receiver does NOT function properly when he 11.____

    A. transmits feedback
    B. files the information
    C. is a poor listener
    D. asks for more information

12. Which one of the following, according to the above passage, is included in the SECOND step of the communication process? 12.____

    A. Selecting the appropriate media to be used in transmission
    B. Formulation of the intended content of the message
    C. Using appropriate media to respond to the receiver's feedback
    D. Transmitting the message through selected channels in the organization

13. The above passage implies that the *decoding process* is MOST NEARLY the reverse of the ______ process. 13.____

    A. transmission
    B. receiving
    C. feedback
    D. encoding

Questions 14-19.

DIRECTIONS: Questions 14 through 19 are to be answered SOLELY on the basis of the following passage.

It is often said that no system will work if the people who carry it out do not want it to work. In too many cases, a departmental reorganization that seemed technically sound and economically practical has proved to be a failure because the planners neglected to take the human factor into account. The truth is that employees are likely to feel threatened when they learn that a major change is in the wind. It does not matter whether or not the change actually poses a threat to an employee; the fact that he believes it does or fears it might is enough to make him feel insecure. Among the dangers he fears, the foremost is the possibility that his job may cease to exist and that he may be laid off or shunted into a less skilled position at lower pay. Even if he knows that his own job category is secure, however, he is likely to fear losing some of the important intangible advantages of his present position–for instance, he may fear that he will be separated from his present companions and thrust in with a group of strangers, or that he will find himself in a lower position on the organizational ladder if a new position is created above his.

It is important that management recognize these natural fears and take them into account in planning any kind of major change. While there is no cut-and-dried formula for preventing employee resistance, there are several steps that can be taken to reduce employees' fears and gain their cooperation. First, unwarranted fears can be dispelled if employees are kept informed of the planning from the start and if they know exactly what to expect. Next, assurance on matters such as retraining, transfers, and placement help should be given as soon as it is clear what direction the reorganization will take. Finally, employees' participation in the planning should be actively sought. There is a great psychological difference between feeling that a change is being forced upon one from the outside, and feeling that one is an insider who is helping to bring about a change.

14. According to the above passage, employees who are not in real danger of losing their jobs because of a proposed reorganization 14.____

A. will be eager to assist in the reorganization
B. will pay little attention to the reorganization
C. should not be taken into account in planning the reorganization
D. are nonetheless likely to feel threatened by the reorganization

15. The passage mentions the *intangible advantages* of a position. 15.____
Which of the following BEST describes the kind of advantages alluded to in the passage?

A. Benefits such as paid holidays and vacations
B. Satisfaction of human needs for things like friendship and status
C. Qualities such as leadership and responsibility
D. A work environment that meets satisfactory standards of health and safety

16. According to the passage, an employee's fear that a reorganization may separate him from his present companions is a (n) 16.____

A. childish and immature reaction to change
B. unrealistic feeling since this is not going to happen

C. possible reaction that the planners should be aware of
D. incentive to employees to participate in the planning

17. On the basis of the above passage, it would be DESIRABLE, when planning a departmental reorganization, to 17.____

A. be governed by employee feelings and attitudes
B. give some employees lower positions
C. keep employees informed
D. lay off those who are less skilled

18. What does the passage say can be done to help gain employees' cooperation in a reorganization? 18.____

A. Making sure that the change is technically sound, that it is economically practical, and that the human factor is taken into account
B. Keeping employees fully informed, offering help in fitting them into new positions, and seeking their participation in the planning
C. Assuring employees that they will not be laid off, that they will not be reassigned to a group of strangers, and that no new positions will be created on the organization ladder
D. Reducing employees' fears, arranging a retraining program, and providing for transfers

19. Which of the following suggested titles would be MOST appropriate for this passage? 19.____

A. PLANNING A DEPARTMENTAL REORGANIZATION
B. WHY EMPLOYEES ARE AFRAID
C. LOOKING AHEAD TO THE FUTURE
D. PLANNING FOR CHANGE: THE HUMAN FACTOR

Questions 20-22.

DIRECTIONS: Questions 20 through 22 are to be answered SOLELY on the basis of the following passage.

The achievement of good human relations is essential if a business office is to produce at top efficiency and is to be a pleasant place in which to work. All office workers plan an important role in handling problems in human relations. They should, therefore, strive to acquire the understanding, tactfulness, and awareness necessary to deal effectively with actual office situations involving co-workers on all levels. Only in this way can they truly become responsible, interested, cooperative, and helpful members of the staff.

20. The selection implies that the MOST important value of good human relations in an office is to develop 20.____

A. efficiency
B. cooperativeness
C. tact
D. pleasantness and efficiency

21. Office workers should acquire understanding in dealing with 21.____

A. co-workers
B. subordinates
C. superiors
D. all members of the staff

22. The selection indicates that a highly competent secretary who is also very argumentative is meeting office requirements 22.____

A. wholly
B. partly
C. slightly
D. not at all

Questions 23-25.

DIRECTIONS: Questions 23 through 25 are to be answered SOLELY on the basis of the following passage.

It is common knowledge that ability to do a particular job and performance on the job do not always go hand in hand. Persons with great potential abilities sometimes fall down on the job because of laziness or lack of interest in the job, while persons with mediocre talents have often achieved excellent results through their industry and their loyalty to the interests of their employers. It is clear; therefore, that in a balanced personnel program, measures of employee ability need to be supplemented by measures of employee performance, for the final test of any employee is his performance on the job.

23. The MOST accurate of the following statements, on the basis of the above paragraph, is that 23.____

A. employees who lack ability are usually not industrious
B. an employee's attitudes are more important than his abilities
C. mediocre employees who are interested in their work are preferable to employees who possess great ability
D. superior capacity for performance should be supplemented with proper attitudes

24. On the basis of the above paragraph, the employee of most value to his employer is NOT necessarily the one who 24.____

A. best understands the significance of his duties
B. achieves excellent results
C. possesses the greatest talents
D. produces the greatest amount of work

25. According to the above paragraph, an employee's efficiency is BEST determined by an 25.____

A. appraisal of his interest in his work
B. evaluation of the work performed by him
C. appraisal of his loyalty to his employer
D. evaluation of his potential ability to perform his work

KEY (CORRECT ANSWERS)

1. B
2. A
3. C
4. C
5. A

6. D
7. A
8. C
9. D
10. B

11. C
12. A
13. D
14. D
15. B

16. C
17. C
18. B
19. D
20. D

21. D
22. B
23. D
24. C
25. B

TEST 3

Questions 1-8.

DIRECTIONS: Questions 1 through 8 are to be answered SOLELY on the basis of the following information and directions.

Assume that you are a clerk in a city agency. Your supervisor has asked you to classify each of the accidents that happened to employees in the agency into the following five categories:

A. An accident that occurred in the period from January through June, between 9 A.M. and 12 Noon, that was the result of carelessness on the part of the injured employee, that caused the employee to lose less than seven working hours, that happened to an employee who was 40 years of age or over, and who was employed in the agency for less than three years;

B. An accident that occurred in the period from July through December, after 1 P.M., that was the result of unsafe conditions, that caused the injured employee to lose less than seven working hours, that happened to an employee who was 40 years of age or over, and who was employed in the agency for three years or more;

C. An accident that occurred in the period from January through June, after 1 P.M., that was the result of carelessness on the part of the injured employee, that caused the injured employee to lose seven or more working hours, that happened to an employee who was less than 40 years old, and who was employed in the agency for three years or more;

D. An accident that occurred in the period from July through December, between 9 A.M. and 12 Noon, that was the result of unsafe conditions, that caused the injured employee to lose seven or more working hours, that happened to an employee who was less than 40 years old, and who was employed in the agency for less than three years;

E. Accidents that cannot be classified in any of the foregoing groups. NOTE: In classifying these accidents, an employee's age and length of service are computed as of the date of accident. In all cases, it is to be assumed that each employee has been employed continuously in city service, and that each employee works seven hours a day, from 9 A.M. to 5 P.M., with lunch from 12 Noon to 1 P.M. In each question, consider only the information which will assist you in classifying the accident. Any information which is of no assistance in classifying an accident should not be considered.

1. The unsafe condition of the stairs in the building caused Miss Perkins to have an accident on October 14, 2003 at 4 P.M. When she returned to work the following day at 1 P.M., Miss Perkins said that the accident was the first one that had occurred to her in her ten years of employment with the agency. She was born on April 27, 1962. 1.____

2. On the day after she completed her six-month probationary period of employment with the agency, Miss Green, who had been considered a careful worker by her supervisor, injured her left foot in an accident caused by her own carelessness. She went home immediately after the accident, which occurred at 10 A.M., March 19, 2004, but returned to work at the regular time on the following morning. Miss Green was born July 12, 1963 in New York City. 2.____

3. The unsafe condition of a duplicating machine caused Mr. Martin to injure himself in an accident on September 8, 2006 at 2 P.M. As a result of the accident, he was unable to work the remainder of the day, but returned to his office ready for work on the following morning. Mr. Martin, who has been working for the agency since April 1, 2003, was born in St. Louis on February 1, 1968. 3.____

4. Mr. Smith was hospitalized for two weeks because of a back injury resulted from an accident on the morning of November 16, 2006. Investigation of the accident revealed that it was caused by the unsafe condition of the floor on which Mr. Smith had been walking. Mr. Smith, who is an accountant, has been anemployee of the agency since March 1, 2004, and was born in Ohio on June 10, 1968. 4.____

5. Mr. Allen cut his right hand because he was careless in operating a multilith machine. Mr. Allen, who was 33 years old when the accident took place, has been employed by the agency since August 17, 1992. The accident, which occurred on January 26, 2006, at 2 P.M., caused Mr. Allen to be absent from work for the rest of the day. He was able to return to work the next morning. 5.____

6. Mr. Rand, who is a college graduate, was born on December, 28, 1967, and has been working for the agency since January 7, 2002. On Monday, April 25, 2005, at 2 P.M., his carelessness in operating a duplicating machine caused him to have an accident and to be sent home from work immediately. Fortunately, he was able to return to work at his regular time on the following Wednesday. 6.____

7. Because he was careless in running down a flight of stairs, Mr. Brown fell, bruising his right hand. Although the accident occurred shortly after he arrived for work on the morning of May 22, 2006, he was unable to resume work until 3 P.M. that day. Mr. Brown was born on August 15, 1955, and began working for the agency on September 12, 2003, as a clerk, at a salary of $22,750 per annum. 7.____

8. On December 5, 2005, four weeks after he had begun working for the agency, the unsafe condition of an automatic stapling machine caused Mr. Thomas to injure himself in an accident. Mr. Thomas, who was born on May 19,1975, lost three working days because of the accident, which occurred at 11:45 A.M. 8.____

Questions 9-10.

DIRECTIONS: Questions 9 and 10 are to be answered SOLELY on the basis of the following paragraph.

An impending reorganization within an agency will mean loss by transfer of several professional staff members from the personnel division. The division chief is asked to designate the persons to be transferred. After reviewing the implications of this reduction of staff with his assistant, the division chief discusses the matter at a staff meeting. He adopts the recommendations of several staff members to have volunteers make up the required reduction.

9. The decision to permit personnel to volunteer for transfer is 9.____

   A. *poor,* it is not likely that the members of a division are of equal value to the division chief
   B. *good;* dissatisfied members will probably be more productive elsewhere
   C. *poor;* the division chief has abdicated his responsibility to carry out the order given to him
   D. *good;* morale among remaining staff is likely to improve in a more cohesive framework

10. Suppose that one of the volunteers is a recently appointed employee who has completed his probationary period acceptably, but whose attitude toward division operations and agency administration tends to be rather negative and sometimes even abrasive. Because of his lack of commitment to the division, his transfer is recommended. If the transfer is approved, the division chief should, prior to the transfer, 10.____

   A. discuss with the staff the importance of commitment to the work of the agency and its relationship with job satisfaction
   B. refrain from any discussion of attitude with the employee
   C. discuss with the employee his concern about the employee's attitude
   D. avoid mention of attitude in the evaluation appraisal prepared for the receiving division chief

Questions 11-16.

DIRECTIONS: Questions 11 through 16 are to be answered SOLELY on the basis of the following paragraph.

Methods of administration of office activities, much of which consists of providing information and *know-how* needed to coordinate both activities within that particular office and other offices, have been among the last to come under the spotlight of management analysis. Progress has been rapid during the past decade, however, and is now accelerating at such a pace that an *information revolution* in office management appears to be in the making. Although triggered by technological breakthroughs in electronic computers and other giant steps in mechanization, this information revolution must be attributed to underlying forces, such as the increased complexity of both governmental and private enterprise, and ever-keener competition. Size, diversification, specialization of function, and decentralization are among the forces which make coordination of activities both more imperative and more difficult. Increased competition, both domestic and international, leaves little margin for error in managerial decisions. Several developments during recent years indicate an evolving pattern. In 1960, the American Management Association expanded the scope of its activities and changed the name of its Office Management Division to Administrative Services Division. Also in 1960, the magazine *Office Management* merged with the magazine *American Business,* and this new publication was named *Administrative Management.*

11. A REASONABLE inference that can be made from the information in the above paragraph is that an important role of the office manager today is to 11.____

A. work toward specialization of functions performed by his subordinates
B. inform and train subordinates regarding any new developments in computer technology and mechanization
C. assist the professional management analysts with the management analysis work in the organization
D. supply information that can be used to help coordinate and manage the other activities of the organization

12. An IMPORTANT reason for the *information revolution* that has been taking place in office management is the 12.____

A. advance made in management analysis in the past decade
B. technological breakthrough in electronic computers and mechanization
C. more competitive and complicated nature of private business and government
D. increased efficiency of office management techniques in the past ten years

13. According to the above paragraph, specialization of function in an organization is MOST likely to result in 13.____

A. the elimination of errors in managerial decisions
B. greater need to coordinate activities
C. more competition with other organizations, both domestic and international
D. a need for office managers with greater flexibility

14. The word *evolving,* as used in the third from last sentence in the above paragraph, means MOST NEARLY 14.____

A. developing by gradual changes
B. passing on to others
C. occurring periodically
D. breaking up into separate, constituent parts

15. Of the following, the MOST reasonable implication of the changes in names mentioned in the last part of the above paragraph is that these groups are attempting to 15.____

A. professionalize the field of office management and the title of Office Manager
B. combine two publications into one because of the increased costs of labor and materials
C. adjust to the fact that the field of office management is broadening
D. appeal to the top managerial people rather than the office management people in business and government

16. According to the above paragraph, intense competition among domestic and international enterprises makes it MOST important for an organization's managerial staff to 16.____

A. coordinate and administer office activities with other activities in the organization
B. make as few errors in decision-making as possible
C. concentrate on decentralization and reduction of size of the individual divisions of the organization
D. restrict decision-making only to top management officials

Questions 17-21.

DIRECTIONS: Questions 17 through 21 are to be answered SOLELY on the basis of the following passage.

For some office workers, it is useful to be familiar with the four main classes of domestic mail; for others, it is essential. Each class has a different rate of postage, and some have requirements concerning wrapping, sealing, or special information to be placed on the package. First class mail, the class which may not be opened for postal inspection, includes letters, postcards, business reply cards, and other kinds of written matter. There are different rates for some of the kinds of cards which can be sent by first class mail. The maximum weight for an item sent by first class mail is 70 pounds. An item which is not letter size should be marked *First Class* on all sides. Although office workers most often come into contact with first class mail, they may find it helpful to know something about the other classes. Second class mail is generally used for mailing newspapers and magazines. Publishers of these articles must meet certain U.S. Postal Service requirements in order to obtain a permit to use second class mailing rates. Third class mail, which must weigh less than 1 pound, includes printed materials and merchandise parcels. There are two rate structures for this class - a single piece rate and a bulk rate. Fourth class mail, also known as parcel post, includes packages weighing from one to 40 pounds. For more information about these classes of mail and the actual mailing rates, contact your local post office.

17. According to this passage, first class mail is the *only* class which 17.____

    A. has a limit on the maximum weight of an item
    B. has different rates for items within the class
    C. may not be opened for postal inspection
    D. should be used by office workers

18. According to this passage, the one of the following items which may CORRECTLY be sent by fourth class mail is a 18.____

    A. magazine weighing one-half pound
    B. package weighing one-half pound
    C. package weighing two pounds
    D. postcard

19. According to this passage, there are different postage rates for 19.____

    A. a newspaper sent by second class mail and a magazine sent by second class mail
    B. each of the classes of mail
    C. each pound of fourth class mail
    D. printed material sent by third class mail and merchandise parcels sent by third class mail

20. In order to send a newspaper by second class mail, a publisher MUST 20.____

    A. have met certain postal requirements and obtained a permit
    B. indicate whether he wants to use the single piece or the bulk rate
    C. make certain that the newspaper weighs less than one pound
    D. mark the newspaper *Second Class* on the top and bottom of the wrapper

21. Of the following types of information, the one which is NOT mentioned in the passage is the 21.____

A. class of mail to which parcel post belongs
B. kinds of items which can be sent by each class of mail
C. maximum weight for an item sent by fourth class mail
D. postage rate for each of the four classes of mail

Questions 22-25.

DIRECTIONS: Questions 22 through 25 are to be answered SOLELY on the basis of the following paragraph.

A standard comprises characteristics attached to an aspect of a process or product by which it can be evaluated. Standardization is the development and adoption of standards. When they are formulated, standards are not usually the product of a single person, but represent the thoughts and ideas of a group, leavened with the knowledge and information which are currently available. Standards which do not meet certain basic requirements become a hindrance rather than an aid to progress. Standards must not only be correct, accurate, and precise in requiring no more and no less than what is needed for satisfactory results, but they must also be workable in the sense that their usefulness is not nullified by external conditions. Standards should also be acceptable to the people who use them. If they are not acceptable, they cannot be considered to be satisfactory, although they may possess all the other essential characteristics.

22. According to the above paragraph, a processing standard that requires the use of materials that cannot be procured is MOST likely to be 22.____

A. incomplete
B. unworkable
C. inaccurate
D. unacceptable

23. According to the above paragraph, the construction of standards to which the performance of job duties should conform is MOST often 23.____

A. the work of the people responsible for seeing that the duties are properly performed
B. accomplished by the person who is best informed about the functions involved
C. the responsibility of the people who are to apply them
D. attributable to the efforts of various informed persons

24. According to the above paragraph, when standards call for finer tolerances than those essential to the conduct of successful production operations, the effect of the standards on the improvement of production operations is 24.____

A. negative
B. negligible
C. nullified
D. beneficial

25. The one of the following which is the MOST suitable title for the above paragraph is 25.____

A. THE EVALUATION OF FORMULATED STANDARDS
B. THE ATTRIBUTES OF SATISFACTORY STANDARDS
C. THE ADOPTION OF ACCEPTABLE STANDARDS
D. THE USE OF PROCESS OR PRODUCT STANDARDS

KEY (CORRECT ANSWERS)

1.	B	11.	D
2.	A	12.	C
3.	E	13.	B
4.	D	14.	A
5.	E	15.	C
6.	C	16.	B
7.	A	17.	C
8.	D	18.	C
9.	A	19.	B
10.	C	20.	A

21.	D
22.	C
23.	D
24.	A
25.	B

READING COMPREHENSION
UNDERSTANDING AND INTERPRETING WRITTEN MATERIAL
EXAMINATION SECTION
TEST 1

DIRECTIONS: Each question or incomplete statement is followed by several suggested answers or completions. Select the one that BEST answers the question or completes the statement. *PRINT THE LETTER OF THE CORRECT ANSWER IN THE SPACE AT THE RIGHT.*

Questions 1-3.

DIRECTIONS: Questions 1 through 3 are to be answered SOLELY on the basis of the following paragraph.

Every organization needs a systematic method of checking its operations as a means to increase efficiency and promote economy. Many successful private firms have instituted a system of audits or internal inspections to accomplish these ends. Law enforcement organizations, which have an extremely important service to *sell,* should be no less zealous in developing efficiency and economy in their operations. Periodic, organized, and systematic inspections are one means of promoting the achievement of these objectives. The necessity of an organized inspection system is perhaps greatest in those law enforcement groups which have grown to such a size that the principal officer can no longer personally supervise or be cognizant of every action taken. Smooth and effective operation demands that the head of the organization have at hand some tool with which he can study and enforce general policies and procedures and also direct compliance with day-to-day orders, most of which are put into execution outside his sight and hearing. A good inspection system can serve as that tool.

1. The central thought of the above paragraph is that a system of inspections within a police department 1.____

   A. is unnecessary for a department in which the principal officer can personally supervise all official actions taken
   B. should be instituted at the first indication that there is any deterioration in job performance by the force
   C. should be decentralized and administered by first-line supervisory officers
   D. is an important aid to the police administrator in the accomplishment of law enforcement objectives

2. The MOST accurate of the following statements concerning the need for an organized inspection system in a law enforcement organization is: It is 2.____

   A. never needed in an organization of small size where the principal officer can give personal supervision
   B. most needed where the size of the organization prevents direct supervision by the principal officer
   C. more needed in law enforcement organizations than in private firms
   D. especially needed in an organization about to embark upon a needed expansion of services

3. According to the above paragraph, the head of the police organization utilizes the internal inspection system 3.____

   A. as a tool which must be constantly re-examined in the light of changing demands for police service
   B. as an administrative technique to increase efficiency and promote economy
   C. by personally visiting those areas of police operation which are outside his sight and hearing
   D. to augment the control of local commanders over detailed field operations

Questions 4-10.

DIRECTIONS: Questions 4 through 10 are to be answered SOLELY on the basis of the following passage.

Job evaluation and job rating systems are intended to introduce scientific procedures. Any type of approach, when properly used, will give satisfactory results. The Point System, when properly validated by actual use, is more likely to be suitable for general use than the ranking system. In many aspects, the Factor Comparison Plan is a point system tied to money values. Of course, there may be another system that combines the ranking system with the point system, especially during the initial stages of the development of the program. After the program has been in use for some time, the tendency is to drop off the ranking phase and continue the use of the point system.

In the ranking system of rating of jobs, every job within the plant is arranged in some order, either from the one with the simplest qualifications to the one with maximum requirements, or in the reverse order. This system should be preceded by careful job analysis and the writing of accurate job descriptions before the rating process is undertaken. It is possible, of course, to take the jobs as they are found in the business enterprise and use the names as they are without any attempt at standardization, and merely rank them according to the general over-all impression of the raters. Such a procedure is certain to fall short of what may reasonably be expected of job rating. Another procedure that is in reality merely a modification of the simple rating described above is to establish a series of grades or zones and arrange all the jobs in the plant into groups within these grades and zones. The practice in most common use is to arrange all the jobs in the plant according to their requirements by rating them and then to establish the classifications or groups.

The actual ranking of jobs may be done by one individual, several individuals, or a committee. If several individuals are working independently on the task, it will usually be found that, in general, they agree but that their rankings vary in certain details. A conference between the individuals, with each person giving his reasons why he rated one way or another, usually produces agreement. The detailed job descriptions are particularly helpful when there is disagreement among raters as to the rating of certain jobs. It is not only possible but desirable to have workers participate in the construction of the job description and in rating the job.

4. The MAIN theme of this passage is 4.____

   A. the elimination of bias in job rating
   B. the rating of jobs by the ranking system

C. the need for accuracy in allocating points in the point system
D. pitfalls to avoid in selecting key jobs in the Factor Comparison Plan

5. The ranking system of rating jobs consists MAINLY of 5.____

A. attaching a point value to each ratable factor of each job prior to establishing an equitable pay scale
B. arranging every job in the organization in descending order and then following this up with a job analysis of the key jobs
C. preparing accurate job descriptions after a job analysis and then arranging all jobs either in ascending or descending order based on job requirements
D. arbitrarily establishing a hierarchy of job classes and grades and then fitting each job into a specific class and grade based on the opinions of unit supervisors

6. The above passage states that the system of classifying jobs MOST used in an organization is to 6.____

A. organize all jobs in the organization in accordance with their requirements and then create categories or clusters of jobs
B. classify all jobs in the organization according to the titles and rank by which they are currently known in the organization
C. establish a pre-arranged series of grades or zones and then fit
D. all jobs into one of the grades or zones
E. determine the salary currently being paid for each job and then rank the jobs in order according to salary

7. According to the above passage, experience has shown that when a group of raters is assigned to the job evaluation task and each individual rates independently of the others, the raters GENERALLY 7.____

A. agree with respect to all aspects of their rankings
B. disagree with respect to all or nearly all aspects of the rankings
C. disagree on overall ratings, but agree on specific rating factors
D. agree on overall rankings, but have some variance in some details

8. The above passage states that the use of a detailed job description is of SPECIAL value when 8.____

A. employees of an organization have participated in the preliminary step involved in actual preparation of the job description
B. labor representatives are not participating in ranking of the jobs
C. an individual rater who is unsure of himself is ranking the jobs
D. a group of raters is having difficulty reaching unanimity with respect to ranking a certain job

9. A comparison of the various rating systems as described in the above passage shows that 9.____

A. the ranking system is not as appropriate for general use as a properly validated point system
B. the point system is the same as the Factor Comparison Plan except that it places greater emphasis on money

C. no system is capable of combining the point system and the Factor Comparison Plan
D. the point system will be discontinued last when used in combination with the Factor Comparison System

10. The above passage implies that the PRINCIPAL reason for creating job evaluation and rating systems was to help 10.____

A. overcome union opposition to existing salary plans
B. base wage determination on a more objective and orderly foundation
C. eliminate personal bias on the part of the trained scientific job evaluators
D. management determine if it was overpricing the various jobs in the organizational hierarchy

Questions 11-13.

DIRECTIONS: Questions 11 through 13 are to be answered SOLELY on the basis of the following paragraph.

The common sense character of the merit system seems so natural to most Americans that many people wonder why it should ever have been inoperative. After all, the American economic system, the most phenomenal the world has ever known, is also founded on a rugged selective process which emphasizes the personal qualities of capacity, industriousness, and productivity. The criteria may not have always been appropriate and competition has not always been fair, but competition there was, and the responsibilities and the rewards – with exceptions, of course – have gone to those who could measure up in terms of intelligence, knowledge, or perseverance. This has been true not only in the economic area, in the money-making process, but also in achievement in the professions and other walks of life.

11. According to the above paragraph, economic rewards in the United States have 11.____

A. always been based on appropriate, fair criteria
B. only recently been based on a competitive system
C. not gone to people who compete too ruggedly
D. usually gone to those people with intelligence, knowledge, and perseverance

12. According to the above passage, a merit system is 12.____

A. an unfair criterion on which to base rewards
B. unnatural to anyone who is not American
C. based only on common sense
D. based on the same principles as the American economic system

13. According to the above passage, it is MOST accurate to say that 13.____

A. the United States has always had a civil service merit system
B. civil service employees are very rugged
C. the American economic system has always been based on a merit objective
D. competition is unique to the American way of life

Questions 14-15.

DIRECTIONS: Questions 14 and 15 are to be answered SOLELY on the basis of the following paragraph.

In-basket tests are often used to assess managerial potential. The exercise consists of a set of papers that would be likely to be found in the in-basket of an administrator or manager at any given time, and requires the individuals participating in the examination to indicate how they would dispose of each item found in the in-basket. In order to handle the in-basket effectively, they must successfully manage their time, refer and assign some work to subordinates, juggle potentially conflicting appointments and meetings, and arrange for follow-up of problems generated by the items in the in-basket. In other words, the in-basket test is attempting to evaluate the participants' abilities to organize their work, set priorities, delegate, control, and make decisions.

14. According to the above paragraph, to succeed in an in-basket test, an administrator must 14.____

   A. be able to read very quickly
   B. have a great deal of technical knowledge
   C. know when to delegate work
   D. arrange a lot of appointments and meetings

15. According to the above paragraph, all of the following abilities are indications of managerial potential EXCEPT the ability to 15.____

   A. organize and control
   B. manage time
   C. write effective reports
   D. make appropriate decisions

Questions 16-19.

DIRECTIONS: Questions 16 through 19 are to be answered SOLELY on the basis of the following paragraph.

A personnel researcher has at his disposal various approaches for obtaining information, analyzing it, and arriving at conclusions that have value in predicting and affecting the behavior of people at work. The type of method to be used depends on such factors as the nature of the research problem, the available data, and the attitudes of those people being studied to the various kinds of approaches. While the experimental approach, with its use of control groups, is the most refined type of study, there are others that are often found useful in personnel research. Surveys, in which the researcher obtains facts on a problem from a variety of sources, are employed in research on wages, fringe benefits, and labor relations. Historical studies are used to trace the development of problems in order to understand them better and to isolate possible causative factors. Case studies are generally developed to explore all the details of a particular problem that is representative of other similar problems. A researcher chooses the most appropriate form of study for the problem he is investigating. He should recognize, however, that the experimental method, commonly referred to as the scientific method, if used validly and reliably, gives the most conclusive results.

16. The above paragraph discusses several approaches used to obtain information on particular problems. Which of the following may be MOST reasonably concluded from the paragraph?
   A(n) 16.____

A. historical study cannot determine causative factors
B. survey is often used in research on fringe benefits
C. case study is usually used to explore a problem that is unique and unrelated to other problems
D. experimental study is used when the scientific approach to a problem fails

17. According to the above paragraph, all of the following are factors that may determine the type of approach a researcher uses EXCEPT 17.____

A. the attitudes of people toward being used in control groups
B. the number of available sources
C. his desire to isolate possible causative factors
D. the degree of accuracy he requires

18. The words *scientific method*, as used in the last sentence of the above paragraph, refer to a type of study which, according to the above paragraph 18.____

A. uses a variety of sources
B. traces the development of problems
C. uses control groups
D. analyzes the details of a representative problem

19. Which of the following can be MOST reasonably concluded from the above paragraph? In obtaining and analyzing information on a particular problem, a researcher employs the method which is the 19.____

A. most accurate
B. most suitable
C. least expensive
D. least time-consuming

Questions 20-25.

DIRECTIONS: Questions 20 through 25 are to be answered SOLELY on the basis of the following passage.

The quality of the voice of a worker is an important factor in conveying to clients and co-workers his attitude and, to some degree, his character. The human voice, when not consciously disguised, may reflect a person's mood, temper, and personality. It has been shown in several experiments that certain character traits can be assessed with better than chance accuracy through listening to the voice of an unknown person who cannot be seen.

Since one of the objectives of the worker is to put clients at ease and to present an encouraging and comfortable atmosphere, a harsh, shrill, or loud voice could have a negative effect. A client who displays emotions of anger or resentment would probably be provoked even further by a caustic tone. In a face-to-face situation, an unpleasant voice may be compensated for, to some degree, by a concerned and kind facial expression. However, when one speaks on the telephone, the expression on one's face cannot be seen by the listener. A supervising clerk who wishes to represent himself effectively to clients should try to eliminate as many faults as possible in striving to develop desirable voice qualities.

20. If a worker uses a sarcastic tone while interviewing a resentful client, the client, according to the above passage, would MOST likely 20.____

A. avoid the face-to-face situation
B. be ashamed of his behavior
C. become more resentful
D. be provoked to violence

21. According to the passage, experiments comparing voice and character traits have demonstrated that 21.____

A. prospects for improving an unpleasant voice through training are better than chance
B. the voice can be altered to project many different psychological characteristics
C. the quality of the human voice reveals more about the speaker than his words do
D. the speaker's voice tells the hearer something about the speaker's personality

22. Which of the following, according to the above passage, is a person's voice MOST likely to reveal? 22.____
His

A. prejudices
B. intelligence
C. social awareness
D. temperament

23. It may be MOST reasonably concluded from the above passage that an interested and sympathetic expression on the face of a worker 23.____

A. may induce a client to feel certain he will receive welfare benefits
B. will eliminate the need for pleasant vocal qualities in the interviewer
C. may help to make up for an unpleasant voice in the interviewer
D. is desirable as the interviewer speaks on the telephone to a client

24. Of the following, the MOST reasonable implication of the above paragraph is that a worker should, when speaking to a client, control and use his voice to 24.____

A. simulate a feeling of interest in the problems of the client
B. express his emotions directly and adequately
C. help produce in the client a sense of comfort and security
D. reflect his own true personality

25. It may be concluded from the above passage that the PARTICULAR reason for a worker to pay special attention to modulating her voice when talking on the phone to a client is that, during a telephone conversation, 25.____

A. there is a necessity to compensate for the way in which a telephone distorts the voice
B. the voice of the worker is a reflection of her mood and character
C. the client can react only on the basis of the voice and words she hears
D. the client may have difficulty getting a clear under-standing over the telephone

KEY (CORRECT ANSWERS)

1.	D	11.	D
2.	B	12.	D
3.	B	13.	C
4.	B	14.	C
5.	C	15.	C
6.	A	16.	B
7.	D	17.	D
8.	D	18.	C
9.	A	19.	B
10.	B	20.	C

21. D
22. D
23. C
24. C
25. C

TEST 2

Questions 1-3.

DIRECTIONS: Questions 1 through 3 are to be answered SOLELY on the basis of the following paragraph.

Suppose you are given the job of printing, collating, and stapling 8,000 copies of a ten-page booklet as soon as possible. You have available one photo-offset machine, a collator with an automatic stapler, and the personnel to operate these machines. All will be available for however long the job takes to complete. The photo-offset machine prints 5,000 impressions an hour, and it takes about 15 minutes to set up a plate. The collator, including time for insertion of pages and stapling, can process about 2,000 booklets an hour. (Answers should be based on the assumption that there are no breakdowns or delays.)

1. Assuming that all the printing is finished before the collating is started, if the job is given to you late Monday and your section can begin work the next day and is able to devote seven hours a day, Monday through Friday, to the job until it is finished, what is the BEST estimate of when the job will be finished? 1.____

   A. Wednesday afternoon of the same week
   B. Thursday morning of the same week
   C. Friday morning of the same week
   D. Monday morning of the next week

2. An operator suggests to you that instead of completing all the printing and then beginning collating and stapling, you first print all the pages for 4,000 booklets, so that they can be collated and stapled while the last 4,000 booklets are being printed. 2.____
   If you accepted this suggestion, the job would be completed

   A. sooner but would require more man-hours
   B. at the same time using either method
   C. later and would require more man-hours
   D. sooner but there would be more wear and tear on the plates

3. Assume that you have the same assignment and equipment as described above, but 16,000 copies of the booklet are needed instead of 8,000. 3.____
   If you decided to print 8,000 complete booklets, then collate and staple them while you started printing the next 8,000 booklets, which of the following statements would MOST accurately describe the relationship between this new method and your original method of printing all the booklets at one time, and then collating and stapling them?
   The

   A. job would be completed at the same time regardless of the method used
   B. new method would result in the job's being completed 3 1/2 hours earlier
   C. original method would result in the job's being completed an hour later
   D. new method would result in the job's being completed 1 1/2 hours earlier.

Questions 4-6.

DIRECTIONS: Questions 4 through 6 are to be answered SOLELY on the basis of the following passage.

When using words like company, association, council, committee, and board in place of the full official name, the writer should not capitalize these short forms unless he intends them to invoke the full force of the institution's authority. In legal contracts, in minutes, or in formal correspondence where one is speaking formally and officially on behalf of the company, the term Company is usually capitalized, but in ordinary usage, where it is not essential to load the short form with this significance, capitalization would be excessive. (Example: The company will have many good openings for graduates this June.)

The treatment recommended for short forms of place names is essentially the same as that recommended for short forms of organizational names. In general, we capitalize the full form but not the short form. If Park Avenue is referred to in one sentence, then the *avenue* is sufficient in subsequent references. The same is true with words like building, hotel, station, and airport, which are capitalized when part of a proper name changed (Pan Am Building, Hotel Plaza, Union Station, O'Hare Airport), but are simply lower-cased when replacing these specific names.

4. The above passage states that USUALLY the short forms of names of organizations 4._____

   A. and places should not be capitalized
   B. and places should be capitalized
   C. should not be capitalized, but the short forms of names of places should be capitalized
   D. should be capitalized, but the short forms of names of places should not be capitalized

5. The above passage states that in legal contracts, in minutes, and in formal correspondence, the short forms of names of organizations should 5._____

   A. usually not be capitalized
   B. usually be capitalized
   C. usually not be used
   D. never be used

6. It can be INFERRED from the above passage that decisions regarding when to capitalize certain words 6._____

   A. should be left to the discretion of the writer
   B. should be based on generally accepted rules
   C. depend on the total number of words capitalized
   D. are of minor importance

Questions 7-10.

DIRECTIONS: Questions 7 through 10 are to be answered SOLELY on the basis of the following passage.

Use of the systems and procedures approach to office management is revolutionizing the supervision of office work. This approach views an enterprise as an entity which seeks to fulfill definite objectives. Systems and procedures help to organize repetitive work into a routine, thus reducing the amount of decision making required for its accomplishment. As a result, employees are guided in their efforts and perform only necessary work. Supervisors are relieved of any details of execution and are free to attend to more important work. Establishing work guides which require that identical tasks be performed the same way each time permits standardization of forms, machine operations, work methods, and controls. This approach also reduces the probability of errors. Any error committed is usually discovered quickly because the incorrect work does not meet the requirement of the work guides. Errors are also reduced through work specialization, which allows each employee to become thoroughly proficient in a particular type of work. Such proficiency also tends to improve the morale of the employees.

7. The above passage states that the accuracy of an employee's work is INCREASED by 7.____

   A. using the work specialization approach
   B. employing a probability sample
   C. requiring him to shift at one time into different types of tasks
   D. having his supervisor check each detail of work execution

8. Of the following, which one BEST expresses the main theme of the above passage? The 8.____

   A. advantages and disadvantages of the systems and procedures approach to office management
   B. effectiveness of the systems and procedures approach to office management in developing skills
   C. systems and procedures approach to office management as it relates to office costs
   D. advantages of the systems and procedures approach to office management for supervisors and office workers

9. Work guides are LEAST likely to be used when 9.____

   A. standardized forms are used
   B. a particular office task is distinct and different from all others
   C. identical tasks are to be performed in identical ways
   D. similar work methods are expected from each employee

10. According to the above passage, when an employee makes a work error, it USUALLY 10.____

   A. is quickly corrected by the supervisor
   B. necessitates a change in the work guides
   C. can be detected quickly if work guides are in use
   D. increases the probability of further errors by that employee

Questions 11-12.

DIRECTIONS: Questions 11 and 12 are to be answered SOLELY on the basis of the following passage.

The coordination of the many activities of a large public agency is absolutely essential. Coordination, as an administrative principle, must be distinguished from and is independent of cooperation. Coordination can be of either the horizontal or the vertical type. In large organizations, the objectives of vertical coordination are achieved by the transmission of orders and statements of policy down through the various levels of authority. It is an accepted generalization that the more authoritarian the organization, the more easily may vertical coordination be accomplished. Horizontal coordination is arrived at through staff work, administrative management, and conferences of administrators of equal rank. It is obvious that of the two types of coordination, the vertical kind is more important, for at best horizontal coordination only supplements the coordination effected up and down the line.

11. According to the above passage, the ease with which vertical coordination is achieved in a large agency depends upon 11.____

A. the extent to which control is firmly exercised from above
B. the objectives that have been established for the agency
C. the importance attached by employees to the orders and statements of policy transmitted through the agency
D. the cooperation obtained at the various levels of authority

12. According to the above passage, 12.____

A. vertical coordination is dependent for its success upon horizontal coordination
B. one type of coordination may work in opposition to the other
C. similar methods may be used to achieve both types of coordination
D. horizontal coordination is at most an addition to vertical coordination

Questions 13-17.

DIRECTIONS: Questions 13 through 17 are to be answered SOLELY on the basis of the following situation.

Assume that you are a newly appointed supervisor in the same unit in which you have been acting as a provisional for some time. You have in your unit the following workers:

WORKER I - He has always been an efficient worker. In a number of his cases, the clients have recently begun to complain that they cannot manage on the departmental budget.

WORKER II - He has been under selective supervision for some time as an experienced, competent worker. He now begins to be late for his supervisory conferences and to stress how much work he has to do.

WORKER III - He has been making considerable improvement in his ability to handle the details of his job. He now tells you, during an individual conference, that he does not need such close supervision and that he wants to operate more independently. He says that Worker II is always available when he needs a little information or help but, in general, he can manage very well by himself.

WORKER IV - He brings you a complex case for decision as to eligibility. Discussion of the case brings out the fact that he has failed to consider all the available resources adequately but has stressed the family's needs to include every extra item in the budget. This is the third case of a similar nature that this worker has brought to you recently. This worker and Worker I work in adjacent territory and are rather friendly.

In the following questions, select the option that describes the method of dealing with these workers that illustrates BEST supervisory practice.

13. With respect to supervision of Worker I, the assistant supervisor should 13.____

A. discuss with the worker, in an individual conference, any problems that he may be having due to the increase in the cost of living
B. plan a group conference for the unit around budgeting, as both Workers I and IV seem to be having budgetary difficulties
C. discuss with Workers I and IV together the meaning of money as acceptance or rejection to the clients
D. discuss with Worker I the budgetary data in each case in relation to each client's situation

14. With respect to supervision of Worker II, the supervisor should 14.____

A. move slowly with this worker and give him time to learn that the supervisor's official appointment has not changed his attitudes or methods of supervision
B. discuss the worker's change of attitude and ask him to analyze the reasons for his change in behavior
C. take time to show the worker how he is avoiding his responsibility in the supervisor-worker relationship and that he is resisting supervision
D. hold an evaluatory conference with the worker and show him how he is taking over responsibilities that are not his by providing supervision for Worker III

15. With respect to supervision of Worker III, the supervisor should discuss with this worker 15.____

A. why he would rather have supervision from Worker II than from the supervisor
B. the necessity for further improvement before he can go on selective supervision
C. an analysis of the improvement that has been made and the extent to which the worker is able to handle the total job for which he is responsible
D. the responsibility of the supervisor to see that clients receive adequate service

16. With respect to supervision of Worker IV, the supervisor should 16.____

A. show the worker that resources figures are incomplete but that even if they were complete, the family would probably be eligible for assistance
B. ask the worker why he is so protective of these families since there are three cases so similar
C. discuss with the worker all three cases at the same time so that the worker may see his own role in the three situations
D. discuss with the worker the reasons for departmental policies and procedures around budgeting

17. With respect to supervision of Workers I and IV, since these two workers are friends and would seem to be influencing each other, the supervisor should 17.____

A. hold a joint conference with them both, pointing out how they should clear with the supervisor and not make their own rules together
B. handle the problems of each separately in individual conferences
C. separate them by transferring one to another territory or another unit
D. take up the problem of workers asking help of each other rather than from the supervisor in a group meeting

Questions 18-20.

DIRECTIONS: Questions 18 through 20 are to be answered SOLELY on the basis of the following passage.

One of the key supervisory problems in a large municipal recreation department is that many leaders are assigned to isolated playgrounds or small centers, where it is difficult to observe their work regularly. Often their facilities are extremely limited. In such settings, as well as in larger recreation centers, where many recreation leaders tend to have other jobs as well, there tends to be a low level of morale and incentive. Still, it is the supervisor's task to help recreation personnel to develop pride in their work and to maintain a high level of performance. With isolated leaders, the supervisor may give advice or assistance. Leaders may be assigned to different tasks or settings during the year to maximize their productivity and provide new challenges. When it is clear that leaders are not willing to make a real effort to contribute to the department, the possibility of penalties must be considered, within the scope of departmental policy and the union contract. However, the supervisor should be constructive, encourage and assist workers to take a greater interest in their work, be innovative, and try to raise morale and to improve performance in positive ways.

18. The one of the following that would be the MOST appropriate title for the above passage is 18.____

A. SMALL COMMUNITY CENTERS - PRO AND CON
B. PLANNING BETTER RECREATION PROGRAMS
C. THE SUPERVISOR'S TASK IN UPGRADING PERSONNEL PERFORMANCE
D. THE SUPERVISOR AND THE MUNICIPAL UNION - RIGHTS AND OBLIGATIONS

19. The above passage makes clear that recreation leadership performance in ALL recreation playgrounds and centers throughout a large city is 19.____

A. generally above average, with good morale on the part of most recreation leaders
B. beyond description since no one has ever observed or evaluated recreation leaders
C. a key test of the personnel department's effort to develop more effective hiring standards
D. of mixed quality, with many recreation leaders having poor morale and a low level of achievement

20. According to the above passage, the supervisor's role is to 20.____

A. use disciplinary action as his major tool in upgrading performance
B. tolerate the lack of effort of individual employees since they are assigned to isolated playgrounds or small centers
C. employ encouragement, advice, and, when appropriate, disciplinary action to improve performance
D. inform the county supervisor whenever malfeasance or idleness is detected

Questions 21-25.

DIRECTIONS: Questions 21 through 25 are to be answered SOLELY on the basis of the following passage.

EMPLOYEE LEAVE REGULATIONS

Peter Smith, as a full-time permanent city employee under the Career and Salary Plan, earns an *annual leave allowance*. This consists of a certain number of days off a year with pay and may be used for vacation, personal business, and for observing religious holidays. As a newly appointed employee, during his first 8 years of city service, he will earn an annual leave allowance of 20 days off a year (an average of 1 2/3 days off a month). After he has finished 8 full years of working for the city, he will begin earning an additional 5 days off a year. His *annual leave allowance*, therefore, will then be 25 days a year and will remain at this amount for seven full years. He will begin earning an additional two days off a year after he has completed a total of 15 years of city employment. Therefore, in his sixteenth year of working for the city, Mr. Smith will be earning 27 days off a year as his *annual leave allowance* (an average of 2 1/4 days off a month).

A sick leave allowance of one day a month is also given to Mr. Smith, but it can be used only in cases of actual illness. When Mr. Smith returns to work after *using sick leave allowance*, he must have a doctor's note if the absence is for a total of more than 3 days, but he may also be required to show a doctor's note for absences of 1, 2, or 3 days.

21. According to the above passage, Mr. Smith's *annual leave allowance* consists of a certain number of days off a year which he 21.____

 A. does not get paid for
 B. gets paid for at time and a half
 C. may use for personal business
 D. may not use for observing religious holidays

22. According to the above passage, after Mr. Smith has been working for the city for 9 years, his *annual leave allowance* will be ______ days a year. 22.____

 A. 20 B. 25 C. 27 D. 37

23. According to the above passage, Mr. Smith will begin earning an average of 2 days off a month as his *annual leave allowance* after he has worked for the city for full years. 23.____

 A. 7 B. 8 C. 15 D. 17

24. According to the above passage, Mr. Smith is given a *sick leave allowance* of 24.____

 A. 1 day every 2 months
 B. 1 day per month
 C. 1 2/3 days per month
 D. 2 1/4 days a month

25. According to the above passage, when he uses *sick leave allowance*, Mr. Smith may be required to show a doctor's note 25.____

 A. even if his absence is for only 1 day
 B. only if his absence is for more than 2 days
 C. only if his absence is for more than 3 days
 D. only if his absence is for 3 days or more

KEY (CORRECT ANSWERS)

1. C
2. C
3. D
4. A
5. B
6. B
7. A
8. D
9. B
10. C
11. A
12. D
13. D
14. A
15. C
16. C
17. B
18. C
19. D
20. C
21. C
22. B
23. C
24. B
25. A

TEST 3

Questions 1-6.

DIRECTIONS: Questions 1 through 6 are to be answered SOLELY on the basis of the following passage.

A folder is made of a sheet of heavy paper (manila, kraft, pressboard, or red rope stock) that has been folded once so that the back is about one-half inch higher than the front. Folders are larger than the papers they contain in order to protect them. Two standard folder sizes are *letter size* for papers that are 8 1/2" x 11" and *legal cap* for papers that are 8 1/2" x 13".

Folders are cut across the top in two ways: so that the back is straight (straight-cut) or so that the back has a tab that projects above the top of the folder. Such tabs bear captions that identify the contents of each folder. Tabs vary in width and position. The tabs of a set of folders that are *one-half cut* are half the width of the folder and have only two positions.

One-third cut folders have three positions, each tab occupying a third of the width of the folder. Another standard tabbing is *one-fifth cut*, which has five positions. There are also folders with *two-fifths cut*, with the tabs in the third and fourth or fourth and fifth positions.

1. Of the following, the BEST title for the above passage is 1.____

   A. FILING FOLDERS
   B. STANDARD FOLDER SIZES
   C. THE USES OF THE FOLDER
   D. THE USE OF TABS

2. According to the above passage, one of the standard folder sizes is called 2.____

   A. Kraft cut
   B. legal cap
   C. one-half cut
   D. straight-cut

3. According to the above passage, tabs are GENERALLY placed along the _______ of the folder. 3.____

   A. back
   B. front
   C. left side
   D. right side

4. According to the above passage, a tab is GENERALLY used to 4.____

   A. distinguish between standard folder sizes
   B. identify the contents of a folder
   C. increase the size of the folder
   D. protect the papers within the folder

5. According to the above passage, a folder that is two-fifths cut has _______ tabs. 5.____

   A. no
   B. two
   C. three
   D. five

6. According to the above passage, one reason for making folders larger than the papers they contain is that 6.____

   A. only a certain size folder can be made from heavy paper
   B. they will protect the papers
   C. they will aid in setting up a tab system
   D. the back of the folder must be higher than the front

Questions 7-15.

DIRECTIONS: Questions 7 through 15 are to be answered SOLELY on the basis of the following passage.

The City University of New York traces its origins to 1847, when the Free Academy, which later became City College, was founded as the first tuition-free municipal college. City and Hunter Colleges were placed under the direction of the Board of Higher Education in 1926, and Brooklyn and Queens Colleges were subsequently added to the system of municipal colleges. In 1955, Staten Island Community College, the first of the two-year colleges sponsored by the Board of Higher Education under the program of the State University of New York, joined the system.

In 1961, the four senior colleges and three community colleges then under the jurisdiction of the Board of Higher Education became the City University of New York, and a University Graduate Division was organized to offer programs leading to the Ph.D. Since then, the university has undergone even more rapid growth. Today, it consists of nine senior colleges, an upper division college which admits students at the junior level, eight community colleges, a graduate division, and an affiliated medical center.

In the summer of 1969, the Board of Higher Education resolved that the time had come to commit the resources of the university to meeting an urgent social need—unrestricted access to higher education for all youths of the City. Determined to prevent the waste of human potential represented by the thousands of high school graduates whose limited educational opportunities left them unable to meet existing admission standards, the Board moved to adopt a policy of Open Admissions. It was their judgment that the best way of determining whether a potential student can benefit from college work is to admit him to college, provide him with the learning assistance he needs, and then evaluate his performance.

Beginning with the class of June 1970, every New York City resident who received a high school diploma from a public or private high school was guaranteed a place in one of the colleges of City University.

7. Of the following, the BEST title for the above passage is 7.____

   A. A BRIEF HISTORY OF THE CITY UNIVERSITY
   B. HIGH SCHOOLS AND THE CITY UNIVERSITY
   C. THE COMPONENTS OF THE UNIVERSITY
   D. TUITION-FREE COLLEGES

8. According to the above passage, which one of the following colleges of the City University was ORIGINALLY called the Free Academy? 8.____

   A. Brooklyn College
   B. City College
   C. Hunter College
   D. Queens College

9. According to the above passage, the system of municipal colleges became the City University of New York in 9.____

   A. 1926
   B. 1955
   C. 1961
   D. 1969

10. According to the above passage, Staten Island Community College came under the jurisdiction of the Board of Higher Education 10.____

A. 6 years after a Graduate Division was organized
B. 8 years before the adoption of the Open Admissions Policy
C. 29 years after Brooklyn and Queens Colleges
D. 29 years after City and Hunter Colleges

11. According to the above passage, the Staten Island Community College is 11.____

A. a graduate division center
B. a senior college
C. a two-year college
D. an upper division college

12. According to the above passage, the TOTAL number of colleges, divisions, and affiliated branches of the City University is 12.____

A. 18 B. 19 C. 20 D. 21

13. According to the above passage, the Open Admissions Policy is designed to determine whether a potential student will benefit from college by PRIMARILY 13.____

A. discouraging competition for placement in the City University among high school students
B. evaluating his performance after entry into college
C. lowering admission standards
D. providing learning assistance before entry into college

14. According to the above passage, the FIRST class to be affected by the Open Admissions Policy was the 14.____

A. high school class which graduated in January 1970
B. City University class which graduated in June 1970
C. high school class when graduated in June 1970
D. City University class which graduated in June 1970

15. According to the above passage, one of the reasons that the Board of Higher Education initiated the policy of Open Admissions was to 15.____

A. enable high school graduates with a background of limited educational opportunities to enter college
B. expand the growth of the City University so as to increase the number and variety of degrees offered
C. provide a social resource to the qualified youth of the City
D. revise admission standards to meet the needs of the City

Questions 16-18.

DIRECTIONS: Questions 16 through 18 are to be answered SOLELY on the basis of the following passage.

Hereafter, all probationary students interested in transferring to community college career programs (associate degrees) from liberal arts programs in senior colleges (bachelor degrees) will be eligible for such transfers if they have completed no more than three semesters.

For students with averages of 1.5 or above, transfer will be automatic. Those with 1.0 to 1.5 averages can transfer provisionally and will be required to make substantial progress during the first semester in the career program. Once transfer has taken place, only those courses in which passing grades were received will be computed in the community college grade-point average.

No request for transfer will be accepted from probationary students wishing to enter the liberal arts programs at the community college.

16. According to this passage, the one of the following which is the BEST statement concerning the transfer of probationary students is that a probationary student 16.____

    A. may transfer to a career program at the end of one semester
    B. must complete three semester hours before he is eligible for transfer
    C. is not eligible to transfer to a career program
    D. is eligible to transfer to a liberal arts program

17. Which of the following is the BEST statement of academic evaluation for transfer purposes in the case of probationary students? 17.____

    A. No probationary student with an average under 1.5 may transfer.
    B. A probationary student with an average of 1.3 may not transfer.
    C. A probationary student with an average of 1.6 may transfer.
    D. A probationary student with an average of .8 may transfer on a provisional basis.

18. It is MOST likely that, of the following, the next degree sought by one who already holds the Associate in Science degree would be a(n) 18.____

    A. Assistantship in Science degree
    B. Associate in Applied Science degree
    C. Bachelor of Science degree
    D. Doctor of Philosophy degree

Questions 19-20.

DIRECTIONS: Questions 19 and 20 are to be answered SOLELY on the basis of the following passage.

Auto: Auto travel requires prior approval by the President and/or appropriate Dean and must be indicated in the *Request for Travel Authorization* form. Employees authorized to use personal autos on official College business will be reimbursed at the rate of 28¢ per mile for the first 500 miles driven and 18¢ per mile for mileage driven in excess of 500 miles. The Comptroller's Office may limit the amount of reimbursement to the expenditure that would have been made if a less expensive mode of transportation (railroad, airplane, bus, etc.) had been utilized. If this occurs, the traveler will have to pick up the excess expenditure as a personal expense.

Tolls, Parking Fees, and Parking Meter Fees are not reimbursable and may not be claimed.

19. Suppose that Professor T. gives the office assistant the following memorandum: 19.____
Used car for official trip to Albany, New York, and return. Distance from New York to Albany is 148 miles. Tolls were $3.50 each way. Parking garage cost $3.00.
When preparing the Travel Expense Voucher for Professor T., the figure which should be claimed for transportation is

A. $120.88 B. $113.88 C. $82.88 D. $51.44

20. Suppose that Professor V. gives the office assistant the following memorandum: 20.____
Used car for official trip to Pittsburgh, Pennsylvania, and return.
Distance from New York to Pittsburgh is 350 miles. Tolls were $3.30, $11.40 going, and $3.30, $2.00 returning.
When preparing the Travel Expense Voucher for Professor V., the figure which should be claimed for transportation is

A. $225.40 B. $176.00 C. $127.40 D. $98.00

Questions 21-25.

DIRECTIONS: Questions 21 through 25 are to be answered SOLELY on the basis of the following passage.

For a period of nearly fifteen years, beginning in the mid-1950's, higher education sustained a phenomenal rate of growth. The factors principally responsible were continuing improvement in the rate of college entrance by high school graduates, a 50 percent increase in the size of the college-age (eighteen to twenty-one) group, and–until about 1967–a rapid expansion of university research activity supported by the Federal government.

Today, as one looks ahead to the year 2010, it is apparent that each of these favorable stimuli will either be abated or turn into a negative factor. The rate of growth of the college-age group has already diminished; and from 2000 to 2005, the size of the college-age group has shrunk annually almost as fast as it grew from 1965 to 1970. From 2005 to 2010, this annual decrease will slow down so that by 2010 the age group will be about the same size as it was in 2009. This substantial net decrease in the size of the college-age group (from 1995 to 2010) will dramatically affect college enrollments since, currently, 83 percent of undergraduates are twenty-one and under, and another 11 percent are twenty-two to twenty-four.

21. Which one of the following factors is NOT mentioned in the above passage as contributing to the high rate of growth of higher education? 21.____

A. A large increase in the size of the eighteen to twenty-one age group
B. The equalization of educational opportunities among socio-economic groups
C. The Federal budget impact on research and development spending in the higher education sector
D. The increasing rate at which high school graduates enter college

22. Based on the information in the above passage, the size of the college-age group in 2010 will be 22.____

A. larger than it was in 2009
B. larger than it was in 1995
C. smaller than it was in 2005
D. about the same as it was in 2000

23. According to the above passage, the tremendous rate of growth of higher education started around 23.____

A. 1950 B. 1955 C. 1960 D. 1965

24. The percentage of undergraduates who are over age 24 is MOST NEARLY 24.____

A. 6% B. 8% C. 11% D. 17%

25. Which one of the following conclusions can be substantiated by the information given in the above passage? 25.____

A. The college-age group was about the same size in 2000 as it was in 1965.
B. The annual decrease in the size of the college-age group from 2000 to 2005 is about the same as the annual increase from 1965 to 1970.
C. The overall decrease in the size of the college-age group from 2000 to 2005 will be followed by an overall increase in its size from 2005 to 2010.
D. The size of the college-age group is decreasing at a fairly constant rate from 1995 to 2010.

KEY (CORRECT ANSWERS)

1. A
2. B
3. A
4. B
5. B
6. B
7. A
8. B
9. C
10. D
11. C
12. C
13. B
14. C
15. A
16. A
17. C
18. C
19. C
20. B
21. B
22. C
23. B
24. A
25. B

NAME and NUMBER COMPARISONS

COMMENTARY

This test seeks to measure your ability and disposition to do a job carefully and accurately, your attention to exactness and preciseness of detail, your alertness and versatility in discerning similarities and differences between things, and your power in systematically handling written language symbols.

It is actually a test of your ability to do academic and/or clerical work, using the basic elements of verbal (qualitative) and mathematical (quantitative) learning - words <u>and</u> numbers.

EXAMINATION SECTION
TEST 1

DIRECTIONS: In each line across the page there are three names or numbers that are much alike. Compare the three names or numbers and decide which ones are exactly alike. *PRINT IN THE SPACE AT THE RIGHT THE LETTER:*

A. if all THREE names or numbers are exactly ALIKE
B. if only the FIRST and SECOND names or numbers are ALIKE
C. if only the FIRST and THIRD names or numbers are ALIKE
D. if only the SECOND and THIRD names or numbers are ALIKE
E. if ALL THREE names or numbers are DIFFERENT

1.	Davis Hazen	David Hozen	David Hazen	1.____
2.	Lois Appel	Lois Appel	Lois Apfel	2.____
3.	June Allan	Jane Allan	Jane Allan	3.____
4.	10235	10235	10235	4.____
5.	32614	32164	32614	5.____

TEST 2

1.	2395890	2395890	2395890	1.____
2.	1926341	1926347	1926314	2.____
3.	E. Owens McVey	E. Owen McVey	E. Owen McVay	3.____
4.	Emily Neal Rouse	Emily Neal Rowse	Emily Neal Rowse	4.____
5.	H. Merritt Audubon	H. Merriott Audubon	H. Merritt Audubon	5.____

TEST 3

1. 6219354	6219354	6219354	1.____
2. 2312793	2312793	2312793	2.____
3. 1065407	1065407	1065047	3.____
4. Francis Ransdell	Frances Ramsdell	Francis Ramsdell	4.____
5. Cornelius Detwiler	Cornelius Detwiler	Cornelius Detwiler	5.____

TEST 4

1. 6452054	6452654	6542054	1.____
2. 8501268	8501268	8501286	2.____
3. Ella Burk Newham	Ella Burk Newnham	Elena Burk Newnham	3.____
4. Jno. K. Ravencroft	Jno. H. Ravencroft	Jno. H. Ravencoft	4.____
5. Martin Wills Pullen	Martin Wills Pulen	Martin Wills Pullen	5.____

TEST 5

1. 3457988	3457986	3457986	1.____
2. 4695682	4695862	4695682	2.____
3. Stricklund Kaneydy	Sticklund Kanedy	Stricklund Kanedy	3.____
4. Joy Harlor Witner	Joy Harloe Witner	Joy Harloe Witner	4.____
5. R.M.O. Uberroth	R.M.O. Uberroth	R.N.O. Uberroth	5.____

TEST 6

1.	1592514	1592574	1592574	1.____
2.	2010202	2010202	2010220	2.____
3.	6177396	6177936	6177396	3.____
4.	Drusilla S. Ridgeley	Drusilla S. Ridgeley	Drusilla S. Ridgeley	4.____
5.	Andrei I. Toumantzev	Andrei I. Tourmantzev	Andrei I. Toumantzov	5.____

TEST 7

1.	5261383	5261383	5261338	1.____
2.	8125690	8126690	8125609	2.____
3.	W.E. Johnston	W.E. Johnson	W.E. Johnson	3.____
4.	Vergil L. Muller	Vergil L. Muller	Vergil L. Muller	4.____
5.	Atherton R. Warde	Asheton R. Warde	Atherton P. Warde	5.____

TEST 8

1.	013469.5	023469.5	02346.95	1.____
2.	33376	333766	333766	2.____
3.	Ling-Temco-Vought	Ling-Tenco-Vought	Ling-Temco Vought	3.____
4.	Lorilard Corp.	Lorillard Corp.	Lorrilard Corp.	4.____
5.	American Agronomics Corporation	American Agronomics Corporation	American Agronomic Corporation	5.____

TEST 9

1.	436592864	436592864	436592864	1.____
2.	197765123	197755123	197755123	2.____
3.	Dewaay, Cortvriendt International S.A.	Deway, Cortvriendt International S.A.	Deway, Corturiendt International S.A.	3.____
4.	Crédit Lyonnais	Crèdit Lyonnais	Crèdit Lyonais	4.____
5.	Algemene Bank Nederland N.V.	Algamene Bank Nederland N.V.	Algemene Bank Naderland N.V.	5.____

TEST 10

1.	00032572	0.0032572	00032522	1.____
2.	399745	399745	398745	2.____
3.	Banca Privata Finanziaria S.p.A.	Banca Privata Finanzaria S.P.A.	Banca Privata Finanziaria S.P.A.	3.____
4.	Eastman Dillon, Union Securities & Co.	Eastman Dillon, Union Securities Co.	Eastman Dillon, Union Securities & Co.	4.____
5.	Arnhold and S. Bleichroeder, Inc.	Arnhold & S. Bleichroeder, Inc.	Arnold and S. Bleichroeder, Inc.	5.____

TEST 11

DIRECTIONS: Answer the questions below on the basis of the following instructions: For each such numbered set of names, addresses and numbers listed in Columns I and II, select your answer from the following options:

A: The names in Columns I and II are different
B: The addresses in Columns I and II are different
C: The numbers in Columns I and II are different
D: The names, addresses and numbers are identical

1.	Francis Jones 62 Stately Avenue 96-12446	Francis Jones 62 Stately Avenue 96-21446	1.____
2.	Julio Montez 19 Ponderosa Road 56-73161	Julio Montez 19 Ponderosa Road 56-71361	2.____
3.	Mary Mitchell 2314 Melbourne Drive 68-92172	Mary Mitchell 2314 Melbourne Drive 68-92172	3.____
4.	Harry Patterson 25 Dunne Street 14-33430	Harry Patterson 25 Dunne Street 14-34330	4.____
5.	Patrick Murphy 171 West Hosmer Street 93-81214	Patrick Murphy 171 West Hosmer Street 93-18214	5.____

TEST 12

1.	August Schultz 816 St. Clair Avenue 53-40149	August Schultz 816 St. Claire Avenue 53-40149	1.____
2.	George Taft 72 Runnymede Street 47-04033	George Taft 72 Runnymede Street 47-04023	2.____
3.	Angus Henderson 1418 Madison Street 81-76375	Angus Henderson 1418 Madison Street 81-76375	3.____
4.	Carolyn Mazur 12 Riven/lew Road 38-99615	Carolyn Mazur 12 Rivervane Road 38-99615	4.____
5.	Adele Russell 1725 Lansing Lane 72-91962	Adela Russell 1725 Lansing Lane 72-91962	5.____

TEST 13

DIRECTIONS: The following questions are based on the instructions given below. In each of the following questions, the 3-line name and address in Column I is the master-list entry, and the 3-line entry in Column II is the information to be checked against the master list.

If there is one line that is *not* exactly alike, mark your answer A.
If there are two lines *not* exactly alike, mark your answer B.
If there are three lines *not* exactly alike, mark your answer C.
If the lines *all are* exactly alike, mark your answer D.

	Column I	Column II	
1.	Jerome A. Jackson 1243 14th Avenue New York, N.Y. 10023	Jerome A. Johnson 1234 14th Avenue New York, N.Y. 10023	1.____
2.	Sophie Strachtheim 33-28 Connecticut Ave. Far Rockaway, N.Y. 11697	Sophie Strachtheim 33-28 Connecticut Ave. Far Rockaway, N.Y. 11697	2.____
3.	Elisabeth NT. Gorrell 256 Exchange St New York, N.Y. 10013	Elizabeth NT. Gorrell 256 Exchange St. New York, N.Y. 10013	3.____
4.	Maria J. Gonzalez 7516 E. Sheepshead Rd. Brooklyn, N.Y. 11240	Maria J. Gonzalez 7516 N. Shepshead Rd. Brooklyn, N.Y. 11240	4.____
5.	Leslie B. Brautenweiler 21-57A Seller Terr. Flushing, N.Y. 11367	Leslie B. Brautenwieler 21-75ASeilerTerr. Flushing, N.J. 11367	5.____

KEYS (CORRECT ANSWERS)

TEST 1	TEST 2	TEST 3	TEST 4	TEST 5	TEST 6	TEST 7
1. E	1. A	1. A	1. E	1. D	1. D	1. B
2. B	2. E	2. A	2. B	2. C	2. B	2. E
3. D	3. E	3. B	3. E	3. E	3. C	3. D
4. A	4. D	4. E	4. E	4. D	4. A	4. A
5. C	5. C	5. A	5. C	5. B	5. E	5. E

TEST 8	TEST 9	TEST 10	TEST 11	TEST 12	TEST 13
1. E	1. A	1. E	1. C	1. B	1. B
2. D	2. D	2. B	2. C	2. C	2. D
3. E	3. E	3. E	3. D	3. D	3. B
4. E	4. E	4. C	4. C	4. B	4. A
5. B	5. E	5. E	5. C	5. A	5. C

NAME AND NUMBER CHECKING

EXAMINATION SECTION
TEST 1

DIRECTIONS: This test is designed to measure your speed/and accuracy. You are urged to work both quickly and accurately and to do correctly as many lists as you can in the time allowed. The test consists of lists of pairs of names and numbers. Count the number of IDENTICAL pairs in each list. Then, select the correct number, 1,2, 3, 4, or 5, and indicate your choice by circling the corresponding number on your answer paper. Two sample questions are presented for your guidance, together with the correct solutions.

SAMPLE QUESTIONS

CIRCLE CORRECT ANSWER

SAMPLE LIST A

Adelphi College - Adelphia College — 1 2 3 4 5
Braxton Corp. - Braxeton Corp.
Wassaic State School - Wassaic State School
Central Islip State Hospital - Central Isllip State Hospital
Greenwich House - Greenwich House

NOTE that there are only two correct pairs - Wassaic State School and Greenwich House. Therefore, the CORRECT answer is 2.

SAMPLE LIST B

78453694	- 78453684	1 2 3 4 5
784530	- 784530	
533	- 534	
67845	- 67845	
2368745	- 2368755	

NOTE that there are only two correct pairs - 784530 and 67845. Therefore, the CORRECT answer is 2.

LIST 1

Diagnostic Clinic	- Diagnostic Clinic	1 2 3 4 5
Yorkville Health	- Yorkville Health	
Meinhard Clinic	- Meinhart Clinic	
Corlears Clinic	- Carlears Clinic	
Tremont Diagnostic	- Tremont Diagnostic	

LIST 2

73526	- 73526	1 2 3 4 5
7283627198	- 7283627198	
627	- 637	
728352617283	- 728352617282	
6281	- 6281	

		CIRCLE CORRECT ANSWER
LIST 3		
Jefferson Clinic	- Jeffersen Clinic	1 2 3 4 5
Mott Haven Center	- Mott Havan Center	
Bronx Hospital	- Bronx Hospital	
Montefiore Hospital	- Montifeore Hospital	
Beth Isreal Hospital	- Beth Israel Hospital	
LIST 4		
936271826	- 936371826	1 2 3 4 5
5271	- 5291	
82637192037	- 82637192037	
527182	- 5271882	
726354256	- 72635456	
LIST 5		
Trinity Hospital	- Trinity Hospital	1 2 3 4 5
Central Harlem	- Centrel Harlem	
St. Luke's Hospital	- St. Lukes' Hospital	
Mt.Sinai Hospital	- Mt.Sinia Hospital	
N.Y.Dispensery	- N.Y.Dispensary	
LIST 6		
725361552637	- 725361555637	1 2 3 4 5
7526378	- 7526377	
6975	- 6975	
82637481028	- 82637481028	
3427	- 3429	
LIST 7		
Misericordia Hospital	- Miseracordia Hospital	1 2 3 4 5
Lebonan Hospital	- Lebanon Hospital	
Gouverneur Hospital	- Gouverner Hospital	
German Polyclinic	- German Policlinic	
French Hospital	- French Hospital	
LIST 8		
8277364933251	- 827364933351	1 2 3 4 5
63728	- 63728	
367281	- 367281	
62733846273	- 6273846293	
62836	- 6283	
LIST 9		
King's County Hospital	- Kings County Hospital	1 2 3 4 5
St.Johns Long Island	- St.John's Long Island	
Bellevue Hospital	- Bellvue Hospital	
Beth David Hospital	- Beth David Hospital	
Samaritan Hospital	- Samariton Hospital	

		CIRCLE CORRECT ANSWER
LIST 10		
62836454	- 62836455	1 2 3 4 5
42738267	- 42738369	
573829	- 573829	
738291627874	- 738291627874	
725	- 735	
LIST 11		
Bloomingdal Clinic	- Bloomingdale Clinic	1 2 3 4 5
Communitty Hospital	- Community Hospital	
Metroplitan Hospital	- Metropoliton Hospital	
Lenox Hill Hospital	- Lonex Hill Hospital	
Lincoln Hospital	- Lincoln Hospital	
LIST 12		
6283364728	- 6283648	1 2 3 4 5
627385	- 627383	
54283902	- 54283602	
63354	- 63354	
7283562781	- 7283562781	
LIST 13		
Sydenham Hospital	- Sydanham Hospital	1 2 3 4 5
Roosevalt Hospital	- Roosevelt Hospital	
Vanderbilt Clinic	- Vanderbild Clinic	
Women's Hospital	- Woman's Hospital	
Flushing Hospital	- Flushing Hospital	
LIST 14		
62738	- 62738	1 2 3 4 5
727355542321	- 72735542321	
263849332	- 263849332	
262837	- 263837	
47382912	- 47382922	
LIST 15		
Episcopal Hospital	- Episcapal Hospital	1 2 3 4 5
Flower Hospital	- Flouer Hospital	
Stuyvesent Clinic	- Stuyvesant Clinic	
Jamaica Clinic	- Jamaica Clinic	
Ridgwood Clinic	- Ridgewood Clinic	
LIST 16		
628367299	- 628367399	1 2 3 4 5
111	- 111	
118293304829	- 1182839489	
4448	- 4448	
333693678	- 333693678	

CIRCLE CORRECT ANSWER

LIST 17

Arietta Crane Farm - Areitta Crane Farm — 1 2 3 4 5
Bikur Chilim Home - Bikur Chilom Home
Burke Foundation - Burke Foundation
Blythedale Home - Blythdale Home
Campbell Cottages - Cambell Cottages

LIST 18

32123 - 32132 — 1 2 3 4 5
273893326783 - 27389326783
473829 - 473829
7382937 - 7383937
362890122332 - 36289012332

LIST 19

Caraline Rest - Caroline Rest — 1 2 3 4 5
Loreto Rest - Loretto Rest
Edgewater Creche - Edgwater Creche
Holiday Farm - Holiday Farm
House of St. Giles - House of st. Giles

LIST 20

557286777 - 55728677 — 1 2 3 4 5
3678902 - 3678892
1567839 - 1567839
7865434712 - 7865344712
9927382 - 9927382

LIST 21

Isabella Home - Isabela Home — 1 2 3 4 5
James A. Moore Home - James A. More Home
The Robin's Nest - The Roben's Nest
Pelham Home - Pelam Home
St.Eleanora's Home - St. Eleanora's Home

LIST 22

273648293048 - 273648293048 — 1 2 3 4 5
334 - 334
7362536478 - 7362536478
7362819273 - 7362819273
7362 - 7363

LIST 23

St.Pheobe's Mission - St.Phebe's Mission — 1 2 3 4 5
Seaside Home - Seaside Home
Speedwell Society - Speedwell Society
Valeria Home - Valera Home
Wiltwyck - Wildwyck

CIRCLE
CORRECT ANSWER

LIST 24

63728	- 63738	1 2 3 4 5
63728192736	- 63728192738	
428	- 458	
62738291527	- 62738291529	
63728192	- 63728192	

LIST 25

McGaffin	- McGafin	1 2 3 4 5
David Ardslee	- David Ardslee	
Axton Supply	- Axeton Supply Co	
Alice Russell	- Alice Russell	
Dobson Mfg.Co.	- Dobsen Mfg. Co.	

KEY (CORRECT ANSWERS)

1. 3
2. 3
3. 1
4. 1
5. 1
6. 2
7. 1
8. 2
9. 1
10. 2
11. 1
12. 2
13. 1
14. 2
15. 1
16. 3
17. 1
18. 1
19. 1
20. 2
21. 1
22. 4
23. 2
24. 1
25. 2

TEST 2

DIRECTIONS: This test is designed to measure your speed and accuracy. You are urged to work both quickly and accurately and to do correctly as many lists as you can in the time allowed. The test consists of lists of pairs of names and numbers. Count the number of IDENTICAL pairs in each list. Then, select the correct number, 1, 2, 3, 4, or 5, and indicate your choice by circling the corresponding number on your answer paper. Two sample questions are presented for your guidance, together with the correct solutions.

CIRCLE CORRECT ANSWER

LIST 1

82637381028	- 82637281028	1 2 3 4 5
928	- 928	
72937281028	- 72937281028	
7362	- 7362	
927382615	- 927382615	

LIST 2

Albee Theatre	- Albee Theatre	1 2 3 4 5
Lapland Lumber Co.	- Laplund Lumber Co.	
Adelphi College	- Adelphi College	
Jones & Son Inc.	- Jones & Sons Inc.	
S.W.Ponds Co.	- S.W. Ponds Co.	

LIST 3

85345	- 85345	1 2 3 4 5
895643278	- 895643277	
726352	- 726353	
632685	- 632685	
7263524	- 7236524	

LIST 4

Eagle Library	- Eagle Library	1 2 3 4 5
Dodge Ltd.	- Dodge Co.	
Stromberg Carlson	- Stromberg Carlsen	
Clairice Ling	- Clairice Linng	
Mason Book Co.	- Matson Book Co.	

LIST 5

66273	- 66273	1 2 3 4 5
629	- 620	
7382517283	- 7382517283	
637281	- 639281	
2738261	- 2788261	

CIRCLE CORRECT ANSWER

LIST 6

Robert MacColl	- Robert McColl	1 2 3 4 5
Buick Motor	- Buck Motors	
Murray Bay & Co.Ltd.	- Murray Bay Co.Ltd.	
L.T. Ltyle	- L.T, Lyttle	
A.S. Landas	- A.S. Landas	

LIST 7

627152637490	- 627152637490	1 2 3 4 5
73526189	- 73526189	
5372	- 5392	
63728142	- 63728124	
4783946	- 4783046	

LIST 8

Tyndall Burke	- Tyndell Burke	1 2 3 4 5
W. Briehl	- W, Briehl	
Burritt Publishing Co.	- Buritt Publishing Co.	
Frederick Breyer & Co.	- Frederick Breyer Co.	
Bailey Buulard	- Bailey Bullard	

LIST 9

634	- 634	1 2 3 4 5
162837	- 163837	
273892223678	- 27389223678	
527182	- 527782	
3628901223	- 3629002223	

LIST 10

Ernest Boas	- Ernest Boas	1 2 3 4 5
Rankin Barne	- Rankin Barnes	
Edward Appley	- Edward Appely	
Camel	- Camel	
Caiger Food Co.	- Caiger Food Co.	

LIST 11

6273	- 6273	1 2 3 4 5
322	- 332	
15672839	- 15672839	
63728192637	- 63728192639	
738	- 738	

LIST 12

Wells Fargo Co.	- Wells Fargo Co.	1 2 3 4 5
W.D. Brett	- W.D. Britt	
Tassco Co.	- Tassko Co.	
Republic Mills	- Republic Mill	
R.W. Burnham	- R.W. Burhnam	

CIRCLE CORRECT ANSWER

LIST 13

7253529152	- 7283529152	1 2 3 4 5
6283	- 6383	
52839102738	- 5283910238	
308	- 398	
82637201927	- 8263720127	

LIST 14

Schumacker Co.	- Shumacker Co.	1 2 3 4 5
C.H. Caiger	- C.H. Caiger	
Abraham Strauss	- Abram Straus	
B.F. Boettjer	- B.F. Boettijer	
Cut-Rate Store	- Cut-Rate Stores	

LIST 15

15273826	- 15273826	1 2 3 4 5
72537	- 73537	
726391027384	- 72639107384	
637389	- 627399	
725382910	- 725382910	

LIST 16

Hixby Ltd.	- Hixby Lt'd.	1 2 3 4 5
S. Reiner	- S. Riener	
Reynard Co.	- Reynord Co.	
Esso Gassoline Co.	- Esso Gasolene Co.	
Belle Brock	- Belle Brock	

LIST 17

7245	- 7245	1 2 3 4 5
819263728192	- 819263728172	
682537289	- 682537298	
789	- 789	
82936542891	- 82936542891	

LIST 18

Joseph Cartwright	- Joseph Cartwrite	1 2 3 4 5
Foote Food Co.	- Foot Food Co.	
Weiman & Held	- Weiman & Held	
Sanderson Shoe Co.	- Sandersen Shoe Co.	
A.M. Byrne	- A.N. Byrne	

LIST 19

4738267	- 4738277	1 2 3 4 5
63728	- 63729	
6283628901	- 6283628991	
918264	- 918264	
263728192037	- 2637728192073	

		CIRCLE CORRECT ANSWER
LIST 20		
Exray Laboratories	- Exray Labratories	1 2 3 4 5
Curley Toy Co.	- Curly Toy Co.	
J. Lauer & Cross	- J. Laeur & Cross	
Mireco Brands	- Mireco Brands	
Sandor Lorand	- Sandor Larand	
LIST 21		
607	- 609	1 2 3 4 5
6405	- 6403	
976	- 996	
101267	- 101267	
2065432	- 20965432	
LIST 22		
John Macy & Sons	- John Macy & Son	1 2 3 4 5
Venus Pencil Co.	- Venus Pencil Co,	
Nell McGinnis	- Nell McGinnis	
McCutcheon & Co.	- McCutcheon & Co.	
Sun-Tan Oil	- Sun-Tan Oil	
LIST 23		
703345700	- 703345700	1 2 3 4 5
46754	- 466754	
3367490	- 3367490	
3379	- 3778	
47384	- 47394	
LIST 24		
arthritis	- athritis	1 2 3 4 5
asthma	- asthma	
endocrene	- endocrene	
gastro-enterological	- gastrol-enteralogical	
orthopedic	- orthopedic	
LIST 25		
743829432	- 743828432	1 2 3 4 5
998	- 998	
732816253902	- 732816252902	
46829	- 46830	
7439120249	- 7439210249	

KEY (CORRECT ANSWERS)

1. 4
2. 3
3. 2
4. 1
5. 2

6. 1
7. 2
8. 1
9. 1
10. 3

11. 3
12. 1
13. 1
14. 1
15. 2

16. 1
17. 3
18. 1
19. 1
20. 1

21. 1
22. 4
23. 2
24. 3
25. 1

NAME AND NUMBER CHECKING

EXAMINATION SECTION
TEST 1

DIRECTIONS: Questions 1 through 17 consist of sets of names and addresses. In each question, the name and address in Column II should be an exact copy of the name and address in Column I.

If there is:
a mistake only in the name, mark your answer A;
a mistake only in the address, mark your answer B;
a mistake in both name and address, mark your answer C;
NO mistake in either name or address, mark your answer D.

SAMPLE QUESTION

Column I	Column II
Christina Magnusson 288 Greene Street New York, N.Y. 10003	Christina Magnusson 288 Greene Street New York, N.Y. 10013

Since there is a mistake only in the address (the zip code should be 10003 instead of 10013), the answer to the sample question is B.

	COLUMN I	COLUMN II	
1.	Ms. Joan Kelly 313 Franklin Ave. Brooklyn, N.Y. 11202	Ms. Joan Kielly 318 Franklin Ave. Brooklyn, N.Y. 11202	1.____
2.	Mrs. Eileen Engel 47-24 86 Road Queens, N.Y. 11122	Mrs. Ellen Engel 47-24 86 Road Queens, N.Y. 11122	2.____
3.	Marcia Michaels 213 E. 81 St. New York, N.Y. 10012	Marcia Michaels 213 E. 81 St. New York, N.Y. 10012	3.____
4.	Rev. Edward J. Smyth 1401 Brandeis Street San Francisco, Calif. 96201	Rev. Edward J. Smyth 1401 Brandies Street San Francisco, Calif. 96201	4.____
5.	Alicia Rodriguez 24-68 81 St. Elmhurst, N.Y. 11122	Alicia Rodriguez 2468 81 St. Elmhurst, N.Y. 11122	5.____
6.	Ernest Eisemann 21 Columbia St. New York, N.Y. 10007	Ernest Eisermann 21 Columbia St. New York, N.Y. 10007	6.____

	Column I	COLUMN II	
7.	Mr. & Mrs. George Petersson 87-11 91st Avenue Woodhaven, N.Y. 11421	Mr. & Mrs. George Peterson 87-11 91st Avenue Woodhaven, N.Y. 11421	7.____
8.	Mr. Ivan Klebnikov 1848 Newkirk Avenue Brooklyn, N.Y. 11226	Mr. Ivan Klebikov 1848 Newkirk Avenue Brooklyn, N.Y. 11622	8.____
9.	Samuel Rothfleisch 71 Pine Street New York, N.Y. 10005	Samuel Rothfleisch 71 Pine Street New York, N.Y. 10005	9.____
10.	Mrs. Isabel Tonnessen 198 East 185th Street Bronx, N.Y. 10458	Mrs. Isabel Tonnessen 189 East 185th Street Bronx, N.Y. 10458	10.____
11.	Esteban Perez 173 Eighth Street Staten Island, N.Y. 10306	Estaban Perez 173 Eighth Street Staten Island, N.Y. 10306	11.____
12.	Esta Wong 141 West 68 St. New York, N.Y. 10023	Esta Wang 141 West 68 St. New York, N.Y. 10023	12.____
13.	Dr. Alberto Grosso 3475 12th Avenue Brooklyn, N.Y. 11218	Dr. Alberto Grosso 3475 12th Avenue Brooklyn, N.Y. 11218	13.____
14.	Mrs. Ruth Bortlas 482 Theresa Ct. Far Rockaway, N.Y. 11691	Ms. Ruth Bortlas 482 Theresa Ct. Far Rockaway, N.Y. 11169	14.____
15.	Mr. & Mrs. Howard Fox 2301 Sedgwick Ave. Bronx, N.Y. 10468	Mr. & Mrs. Howard Fox 231 Sedgwick Ave. Bronx, N.Y. 10468	15.____
16.	Miss Marjorie Black 223 East 23 Street New York, N.Y. 10010	Miss Margorie Black 223 East 23 Street New York, N.Y. 10010	16.____
17.	Michelle Herman 806 Valley Rd. Old Tappan, N.J. 07675	Michelle Hermann 806 Valley Dr. Old Tappan, N.J. 07675	17.____

KEY (CORRECT ANSWERS)

1. C
2. A
3. D
4. B
5. B
6. A
7. A
8. C
9. D
10. B
11. A
12. A
13. D
14. C
15. B
16. A
17. C

TEST 2

DIRECTIONS: Questions 1 through 15 are to be answered SOLELY on the instructions given below. *PRINT THE LETTER OF THE CORRECT ANSWER IN THE SPACE AT THE RIGHT.*

INSTRUCTIONS:

In each of the following questions, the 3-line name and address in Column I is the master-list entry, and the 3-line entry in Column 2 is the information to be checked against the master list. If there is one line that does not match, mark your answer A; if there are two lines that do not match, mark your answer B; if all three lines do not match, mark your answer C; if the lines all match exactly, mark your answer D.

SAMPLE QUESTION

Column I	Column II
Mark L. Field	Mark L. Field
11-09 Prince Park Blvd.	11-99 Prince Park Way
Bronx, N.Y. 11402	Bronx, N.Y. 11401

The first lines in each column match exactly. The second lines do not match since 11-09 does not match 11-99; and Blvd. does not match Way. The third lines do not match either since 11402 does not match 11401. Therefore, there are two lines that do not match, and the CORRECT answer is B.

	COLUMN I	COLUMN II	
1.	Jerome A. Jackson 1243 14th Avenue New York, N.Y. 10023	Jerome A. Johnson 1234 14th Avenue New York, N.Y. 10023	1.___
2.	Sophie Strachtheim 33-28 Connecticut Ave. Far Rockaway, N.Y. 11697	Sophie Strachtheim 33-28 Connecticut Ave. Far Rockaway, N.Y. 11697	2.___
3.	Elisabeth N.T. Gorrell 256 Exchange St. New York, N.Y. 10013	Elizabeth N.T. Gorrell 256 Exchange St. New York, N.Y. 10013	3.___
4.	Maria J. Gonzalez 7516 E. Sheepshead Rd. Brooklyn, N.Y. 11240	Maria J. Gonzalez 7516 N. Shepshead Rd. Brooklyn, N.Y. 11240	4.___
5.	Leslie B. Brautenweiler 21 57A Seiler Terr. Flushing, N.Y. 11367	Leslie B. Brautenwieler 21-75A Seiler Terr. Flushing, N.J. 11367	5.___
6.	Rigoberto J. Peredes 157 Twin Towers, #18F Tottenville, S.I., N.Y.	Rigoberto J. Peredes 157 Twin Towers, #18F Tottenville, S.I., N.Y.	6.___

	COLUMN I	COLUMN II	
7.	Pietro F. Albino P.O. Box 7548 Floral Park, N.Y. 11005	Pietro F. Albina P.O. Box 7458 Floral Park, N.Y. 11005	7.____
8.	Joanne Zimmermann Bldg. SW, Room 314 532-4601	Joanne Zimmermann Bldg. SW, Room 314 532-4601	8.____
9.	Carlyle Whetstone Payroll Div.-A, Room 212A 262-5000, ext. 471	Caryle Whetstone Payroll Div.-A, Room 212A 262-5000, ext. 417	9.____
10.	Kenneth Chiang Legal Council, Room 9745 (201) 416-9100, ext. 17	Kenneth Chiang Legal Counsel, Room 9745 (201) 416-9100, ext. 17	10.____
11.	Ethel Koenig Personnel Services Division, Room 433; 635-7572	Ethel Hoenig Personal Services Division, Room 433; 635-7527	11.____
12.	Joyce Ehrhardt Office of the Administrator, Room W56; 387-8706	Joyce Ehrhart Office of the Administrator, Room W56; 387-7806	12.____
13.	Ruth Lang EAM Bldg., Room C101 625-2000, ext. 765	Ruth Lang EAM Bldg., Room C110 625-2000, ext. 765	13.____
14.	Anne Marie Ionozzi Investigations, Room 827 576-4000, ext. 832	Anna Marie Ionozzi Investigation, Room 827 566-4000, ext. 832	14.____
15.	Willard Jameson Fm C Bldg., Room 687 454-3010	Willard Jamieson Fm C Bldg., Room 687 454-3010	15.____

KEY (CORRECT ANSWERS)

1. B
2. D
3. A
4. A
5. C
6. D
7. B
8. D
9. B
10. A
11. C
12. B
13. A
14. C
15. A

TEST 3

DIRECTIONS: Questions 1 through 10 are to be answered on the basis of the following instructions. *PRINT THE LETTER OF THE CORRECT ANSWER IN THE SPACE AT THE RIGHT.*

INSTRUCTIONS:

For each such set of names, addresses, and numbers listed in Columns I and II, select your answer from the following options:

A. The names in Columns I and II are different.
B. The addresses in Columns I and II are different.
C. The numbers in Columns I and II are different.
D. The names, addresses, and numbers in Columns I and II are identical.

	COLUMN I	COLUMN II	
1.	Francis Jones 62 Stately Avenue 96-12446	Francis Jones 62 Stately Avenue 96-21446	1.____
2.	Julio Montez 19 Ponderosa Road 56-73161	Julio Montez 19 Ponderosa Road 56-71361	2.____
3.	Mary Mitchell 2314 Melbourne Drive 68-92172	Mary Mitchell 2314 Melbourne Drive 68-92172	3.____
4.	Harry Patterson 25 Dunne Street 14-33430	Harry Patterson 25 Dunne Street 14-34330	4.____
5.	Patrick Murphy 171 West Hosmer Street 93-81214	Patrick Murphy 171 West Hosmer Street 93-18214	5.____
6.	August Schultz 816 St. Clair Avenue 53-40149	August Schultz 816 St. Claire Avenue 53-40149	6.____
7.	George Taft 72 Runnymede Street 47-04033	George Taft 72 Runnymede Street 47-04023	7.____
8.	Angus Henderson 1418 Madison Street 81-76375	Angus Henderson 1418 Madison Street 81-76375	8.____
9.	Carolyn Mazur 12 Riverview Road 38-99615	Carolyn Mazur 12 Rivervane ftoad 38-99615	9.____

	COLUMN I	COLUMN II	
10.	Adele Russell 1725 Lansing Lane 72-91962	Adela Russell 1725 Lansing Lane 72-91962	10.____

KEY (CORRECT ANSWERS)

1.	C	6.	B
2.	C	7.	C
3.	D	8.	D
4.	C	9.	B
5.	C	10.	A

TEST 4

DIRECTIONS: Questions 1 through 20 test how good you are at catching mistakes in typing or printing. In each question, the name and address in Column II should be an exact copy of the name and address in Column I. Mark your answer

A. if there is no mistake in either name or address;
B. if there is a mistake in both name and address;
C. if there is a mistake only in the name;
D. if there is a mistake only in the address.

PRINT THE LETTER OF THE CORRECT ANSWER IN THE SPACE AT THE RIGHT.

	COLUMN I	COLUMN II	
1.	Milos Yanocek 33-60 14 Street Long Island City, N.Y. 11011	Milos Yanocek 33-60 14 Street Long Island City, N.Y. 11001	1.____
2.	Alphonse Sabattelo 24 Minnetta Lane New York, N.Y. 10006	Alphonse Sabbattelo 24 Minetta Lane New York, N.Y. 10006	2.____
3.	Helen Steam 5 Metropolitan Oval Bronx, N.Y. 10462	Helene Stearn 5 Metropolitan Oval Bronx, N.Y. 10462	3.____
4.	Jacob Weisman 231 Francis Lewis Boulevard Forest Hills, N.Y. 11325	Jacob Weisman 231 Francis Lewis Boulevard Forest Hills, N.Y. 11325	4.____
5.	Riccardo Fuente 134 West 83 Street New York, N.Y. 10024	Riccardo Fuentes 134 West 88 Street New York, N.Y. 10024	5.____
6.	Dennis Lauber 52 Avenue D Brooklyn, N.Y. 11216	Dennis Lauder 52 Avenue D Brooklyn, N.Y. 11216	6.____
7.	Paul Cutter 195 Galloway Avenue Staten Island, N.Y. 10356	Paul Cutter 175 Galloway Avenue Staten Island, N.Y. 10365	7.____
8.	Sean Donnelly 45-58 41 Avenue Woodside, N.Y. 11168	Sean Donnelly 45-58 41 Avenue Woodside, N.Y. 11168	8.____
9.	Clyde Willot 1483 Rockaway Avenue Brooklyn, N.Y. 11238	Clyde Willat 1483 Rockway Avenue Brooklyn, N.Y. 11238	9.____

	COLUMN I	COLUMN II	
10.	Michael Stanakis 419 Sheriden Avenue Staten Island, N.Y. 10363	Michael Stanakis 419 Sheraden Avenue Staten Island, N.Y. 10363	10.____
11.	Joseph DiSilva 63-84 Saunders Road Rego Park, N.Y. 11431	Joseph Disilva 64-83 Saunders Road Rego Park, N.Y. 11431	11.____
12.	Linda Polansky 2225 Fenton Avenue Bronx, N.Y. 10464	Linda Polansky 2255 Fenton Avenue Bronx, N.Y. 10464	12.____
13.	Alfred Klein 260 Hillside Terrace Staten Island, N.Y. 15545	Alfred Klein 260 Hillside Terrace Staten Island, N.Y. 15545	13.____
14.	William McDonnell 504 E. 55 Street New York, N.Y. 10103	William McConnell 504 E. 55 Street New York, N.Y. 10108	14.____
15.	Angela Cipolla 41-11 Parson Avenue Flushing, N.Y. 11446	Angela Cipola 41-11 Parsons Avenue Flushing, N.Y. 11446	15.____
16.	Julie Sheridan 1212 Ocean Avenue Brooklyn, N.Y. 11237	Julia Sheridan 1212 Ocean Avenue Brooklyn, N.Y. 11237	16.____
17.	Arturo Rodriguez 2156 Cruger Avenue Bronx, N.Y. 10446	Arturo Rodrigues 2156 Cruger Avenue Bronx, N.Y. 10446	17.____
18.	Helen McCabe 2044 East 19 Street Brooklyn, N.Y. 11204	Helen McCabe 2040 East 19 Street Brooklyn,. N.Y. 11204	18.____
19.	Charles Martin 526 West 160 Street New York, N.Y. 10022	Charles Martin 526 West 160 Street New York, N.Y. 10022	19.____
20.	Morris Rabinowitz 31 Avenue M Brooklyn, N.Y. 11216	Morris Rabinowitz 31 Avenue N Brooklyn, N.Y. 11216	20.____

KEY (CORRECT ANSWERS)

1.	D	11.	B
2.	B	12.	D
3.	C	13.	A
4.	A	14.	B
5.	B	15.	B
6.	C	16.	C
7.	D	17.	C
8.	A	18.	D
9.	B	19.	A
10.	D	20.	D

TEST 5

DIRECTIONS: In copying the addresses below from Column A to the same line in Column B, an Agent-in-Training made some errors. For Questions 1 through 5, if you find that the Agent made an error in
only one line, mark your answer A;
only two lines, mark your answer B;
only three lines, mark your answer C;
all four lines, mark your answer D.

EXAMPLE

Column A	Column B
24 Third Avenue	24 Third Avenue
5 Lincoln Road	5 Lincoln Street
50 Central Park West	6 Central Park West
37-21 Queens Boulevard	21-37 Queens Boulevard

Since errors were made on only three lines, namely the second, third, and fourth, the CORRECT answer is C.

PRINT THE LETTER OF THE CORRECT ANSWER IN THE SPACE AT THE RIGHT.

	Column A	Column B	
1.	57-22 Springfield Boulevard	75-22 Springfield Boulevard	1.____
	94 Gun Hill Road	94 Gun Hill Avenue	
	8 New Dorp Lane	8 New Drop Lane	
	36 Bedford Avenue	36 Bedford Avenue	
2.	538 Castle Hill Avenue	538 Castle Hill Avenue	2.____
	54-15 Beach Channel Drive	54-15 Beach Channel Drive	
	21 Ralph Avenue	21 Ralph Avenue	
	162 Madison Avenue	162 Morrison Avenue	
3.	49 Thomas Street	49 Thomas Street	3.____
	27-21 Northern Blvd.	21-27 Northern Blvd.	
	86 125th Street	86 125th Street	
	872 Atlantic Ave.	872 Baltic Ave.	
4.	261-17 Horace Harding Expwy.	261-17 Horace Harding Pkwy.	4.____
	191 Fordham Road	191 Fordham Road	
	6 Victory Blvd.	6 Victoria Blvd.	
	552 Oceanic Ave.	552 Ocean Ave.	
5.	90-05 38th Avenue	90-05 36th Avenue	5.____
	19 Central Park West	19 Central Park East	
	9281 Avenue X	9281 Avenue X	
	22 West Farms Square	22 West Farms Square	

KEY (CORRECT ANSWERS)

1. C
2. A
3. B
4. C
5. B

TEST 6

Questions 1-10.

DIRECTIONS: For Questions 1 through 10, choose the letter in Column II next to the number which EXACTLY matches the number in Column I. *PRINT THE LETTER OF THE CORRECT ANSWER IN THE SPACE AT THE RIGHT.*

COLUMN I	COLUMN II	
1. 14235	A. 13254 B. 12435 C. 13245 D. 14235	1.____
2. 70698	A. 90768 B. 60978 C. 70698 D. 70968	2.____
3. 11698	A. 11689 B. 11986 C. 11968 D. 11698	3.____
4. 50497	A. 50947 B. 50497 C. 50749 D. 54097	4.____
5. 69635	A. 60653 B. 69630 C. 69365 D. 69635	5.____
6. 1201022011	A. 1201022011 B. 1201020211 C. 1202012011 D. 1021202011	6.____
7. 3893981389	A. 3893891389 B. 3983981389 C. 3983891389 D. 3893981389	7.____
8. 4765476589	A. 4765476598 B. 4765476588 C. 4765476589 D. 4765746589	8.____

COLUMN I	COLUMN II	
9. 8679678938	A. 8679687938 B. 8679678938 C. 8697678938 D. 8678678938	9.____
10. 6834836932	A. 6834386932 B. 6834836923 C. 6843836932 D. 6834836932	10.____

Questions 11-15.

DIRECTIONS: For Questions 11 through 15, determine how many of the symbols in Column Z are exactly the same as the symbol in Column Y.
If none is exactly the same, answer A;
if only one symbol is exactly the same, answer B;
if two symbols are exactly the same, answer C;
if three symbols are exactly the same, answer D.

COLUMN Y	COLUMN Z	
11. A123B1266	A123B1366 A123B1266 A133B1366 A123B1266	11.____
12. CC28D3377	CD22D3377 CC38D3377 CC28C3377 CC28D2277	12.____
13. M21AB201X	M12AB201X M21AB201X M21AB201Y M21BA201X	13.____
14. PA383Y744	AP383Y744 PA338Y744 PA388Y744 PA383Y774	14.____
15. PB2Y8893	PB2Y8893 PB2Y8893 PB3Y8898 PB2Y8893	15.____

KEY (CORRECT ANSWERS)

1. D
2. C
3. D
4. B
5. D
6. A
7. D
8. C
9. B
10. D
11. C
12. A
13. B
14. A
15. D

ARITHMETICAL REASONING
EXAMINATION SECTION
TEST 1

DIRECTIONS: Each question or incomplete statement is followed by several suggested answers or completions. Select the one that BEST answers the question or completes the statement. *PRINT THE LETTER OF THE CORRECT ANSWER IN THE SPACE AT THE RIGHT.*

1. If a secretary answered 28 phone calls and typed the addresses for 112 credit statements in one morning, what is the RATIO of phone calls answered to credit statements typed for that period of time? 1.____

   A. 1:4 B. 1:7 C. 2:3 D. 3:5

2. According to a suggested filing system, no more than 10 folders should be filed behind any one file guide and from 15 to 25 file guides should be used in each file drawer for easy finding and filing. 2.____
   The MAXIMUM number of folders that a five-drawer file cabinet can hold to allow easy finding and filing is

   A. 550 B. 750 C. 1,100 D. 1,250

3. An employee had a starting salary of $19,353. He received a salary increase at the end of each year, and at the end of the seventh year his salary was $25,107. 3.____
   What was his AVERAGE annual increase in salary over these seven years?

   A. $765 B. $807 C. $822 D. $858

4. The 55 typists and 28 senior clerks in a certain agency were paid a total of $1,457,400 in salaries in 2005. 4.____
   If the average annual salary of a typist was $16,800, the average annual salary of a senior clerk was

   A. $19,050 B. $19,950 C. $20,100 D. $20,250

5. A typist has been given a three-page report to type. She has finished typing the first two pages. The first page has 283 words, and the second page has 366 words. 5.____
   If the total report consists of 954 words, how many words will she have to type on the third page of the report?

   A. 202 B. 287 C. 305 D. 313

6. In one day, Clerk A processed 30% more forms than Clerk B, and Clerk C processed 1 1/4 as many forms as Clerk A. 6.____
   If Clerk B processed 40 forms, how many more forms were processed by Clerk C than Clerk B?

   A. 12 B. 13 C. 21 D. 25

7. A clerk who earns a gross salary of $678 every 2 weeks has the following deductions taken from her paycheck: 15% for city, state, and federal taxes; 2 1/2% for Social Security; $1.95 for health insurance; and $9.00 for union dues. The amount of her take-home pay is 7.____

A. $429.60 B. $468.60 C. $497.40 D. $548.40

8. In 2002, an agency spent $400 to buy pencils at a cost of $1.00 a dozen. If the agency used 3/4 of these pencils in 2002 and used the same number of pencils in 2003, how many more pencils did it have to buy to have enough pencils for all of 2003? 8.____

A. 1,200 B. 2,400 C. 3,600 D. 4,800

9. A clerk who worked in Agency X earned the following salaries: $15,105 the first year, $15,750 the second year, and $16,440 the third year. Another clerk who worked in Agency Y for three years earned $15,825 a year for two years and $16,086 the third year. The DIFFERENCE between the average salaries received by both clerks over a three-year period is 9.____

A. $147 B. $153 C. $261 D. $423

10. An employee who works more than 40 hours in any week receives overtime payment for the extra hours at time and one-half (1 1/2 times) his hourly rate of pay. An employee who earns $13.60 an hour works a total of 45 hours during a certain week. His TOTAL pay for that week would be 10.____

A. $564.40 B. $612.00 C. $646.00 D. $824.00

11. Suppose that the amount of money spent for supplies in 2006 for a division in a city department was $156,500. This represented an increase of 12% over the amount spent for supplies for this division in 2005. The amount of money spent for supplies for this division in 2005 was MOST NEARLY 11.____

A. $139,730 B. $137,720 C. $143,460 D. $138,720

12. Suppose that a group of five clerks have been assigned to insert 24,000 letters into envelopes. The clerks perform this work at the following rates of speed: Clerk A, 1,100 letters an hour; Clerk B, 1,450 letters an hour; Clerk C, 1,200 letters an hour; Clerk D, 1,300 letters an hour; Clerk E, 1,250 letters an hour. At the end of two hours of work, Clerks C and D are assigned to another task. From the time that Clerks C and D were taken off the assignment, the number of hours required for the remaining clerks to complete this assignment is 12.____

A. less than 3 hours
B. 3 hours
C. more than 3 hours, but less than 4 hours
D. more than 4 hours

13. The number 60 is 40% of 13.____

A. 24 B. 84 C. 96 D. 150

14. If 3/8 of a number is 96, the number is 14.____

A. 132 B. 36 C. 256 D. 156

15. A city department uses an average of 25 20-cent, 35 30-cent, and 350 40-cent postage stamps each day. 15.____
The TOTAL cost of stamps used by the department in a five-day period is

A. $29.50 B. $155.50 C. $290.50 D. $777.50

16. A city department issued 12,000 applications in 2000. The number of applications that the department issued in 1998 was 25% greater than the number it issued in 2000. 16.____
If the department issued 10% fewer applications in 1996 than it did in 1998, the number it issued in 1996 was

A. 16,500 B. 13,500 C. 9,900 D. 8,100

17. A clerk can add 40 columns of figures an hour by using an adding machine and 20 columns of figures an hour without using an adding machine. 17.____
The TOTAL number of hours it would take him to add 200 columns if he does 3/5 of the work by machine and the rest without the machine is

A. 6 B. 7 C. 8 D. 9

18. In 1997, a city department bought 500 dozen pencils at $1.20 per dozen. In 2000, only 75 percent as many pencils were bought as were bought in 1997, but the price was 20 percent higher than the 1997 price. The TOTAL cost of the pencils bought in 2000 was 18.____

A. $540 B. $562.50 C. $720 D. $750

19. A clerk is assigned to check the accuracy of the entries on 490 forms. He checks 40 forms an hour. After working one hour on this task, he is joined by another clerk, who checks these forms at the rate of 35 an hour. 19.____
The TOTAL number of hours required to do the entire assignment is

A. 5 B. 6 C. 7 D. 8

20. Assume that there are a total of 420 employees in a city agency. Thirty percent of the employees are clerks, and 1/7 are typists. 20.____
The DIFFERENCE between the number of clerks and the number of typists is

A. 126 B. 66 C. 186 D. 80

21. Assume that a duplicating machine produces copies of a bulletin at a cost of 2 cents per copy. The machine produces 120 copies of the bulletin per minute. 21.____
If the cost of producing a certain number of copies was $12, how many minutes of operation did it take the machine to produce this number of copies?

A. 5 B. 2 C. 10 D. 6

22. An assignment is completed by 32 clerks in 22 days. Assuming that all the clerks work at the same rate of speed, the number of clerks that would be needed to complete this assignment in 16 days is 22.____

A. 27 B. 38 C. 44 D. 52

23. A department head hired a total of 60 temporary employees to handle a seasonal increase in the department's workload. The following lists the number of temporary employees hired, their rates of pay, and the duration of their employment: 23.____

One-third of the total were hired as clerks, each at the rate of $27,500 a year, for two months.

30 percent of the total were hired as office machine operators, each at the rate of $31,500 a year, for four months.

22 stenographers were hired, each at the rate of $30,000 a year, for three months.

The total amount paid to these temporary employees was MOST NEARLY

A. $1,780,000 B. $450,000
C. $650,000 D. $390,000

24. Assume that there are 2,300 employees in a city agency. Also, assume that five percent of these employees are accountants, that 80 percent of the accountants have college degrees, and that one-half of the accountants who have college degrees have five years of experience. Then, the number of employees in the agency who are accountants with college degrees and five years of experience is 24.____

A. 46 B. 51 C. 460 D. 920

25. Assume that the regular 8-hour working day of a laborer is from 8 A.M. to 5 P.M., with an hour off for lunch. He earns a regular hourly rate of pay for these 8 hours and is paid at the rate of time-and-a-half for each hour worked after his regular working day. 25.____
If, on a certain day, he works from 8 A.M. to 6 P.M., with an hour off for lunch, and earns $171, his regular hourly rate of pay is

A. $16.30 B. $17.10 C. $18.00 D. $19.00

KEY (CORRECT ANSWERS)

1. A
2. D
3. C
4. A
5. C

6. D
7. D
8. B
9. A
10. C

11. A
12. B
13. D
14. C
15. D

16. B
17. B
18. A
19. C
20. B

21. A
22. C
23. B
24. A
25. C

SOLUTIONS TO PROBLEMS

1. 28/112 is equivalent to 1:4
2. Maximum number of folders = (10)(25)(5) = 1250
3. Average annual increase = ($25,107-19,353) ÷ 7 = $822
4. $1,457,400 - (55)($16,800) = $533,400 = total amount paid to senior clerks. Average senior clerk's salary = $533,400 ÷ 28 = $19,050
5. Number of words on 3rd page = 954 - 283 - 366 = 305
6. Clerk A processed (40)(1.30) = 52 forms and clerk C processed (52)(1.25) = 65 forms. Finally, 65 - 40 = 25
7. Take-home pay = $678 - (.15)($678) - (.025)($678) - $1.95 - $9.00 = $548.40
8. (400)(12) = 4800 pencils. In 2002, (3/4)(4800) = 3600 were used, so that 1200 pencils were available at the beginning of 2003. Since 3600 pencils were also used in 2003, the agency had to buy 3600 - 1200 = 2400 pencils.
9. Average salary for clerk in Agency X = ($15,105+$15,750+$16,440)/3 = $15,765. Average salary for clerk in Agency Y = ($15,825+ $15,825+$16,086) ÷ 3 = $15,912. Difference in average salaries = $147.
10. Total pay = ($13.60)(40) + ($20.40)(5) = $646.00
11. In 2005, amount spent = $156,500 ÷ 1.12 ≈ $139,730 (Actual value = $139,732.1429)
12. At the end of 2 hours, (1100)(2) + (1450)(2) + (1200)(2) + (1300X2) + (1250X2) = 12,600 letters have been inserted into envelopes. The remaining 11,400 letters done by clerks A, B, and C will require 11,400 ÷ (1100+1450+1250) = 3 hours.
13. 60 ÷ .40 = 150
14. 96 ÷ 3/8 = (96)(8/3) = 256
15. Total cost = (5)[(25)(.20)+(35)(.30)+(350)(.40)]= $777.50
16. In 1998, (12,000) (1.25) = 15,000 applications were issued In 1996, (15,000)(.90) = 13,500 applications were issued
17. Total number of hours $=\frac{120}{40}+\frac{80}{20}=7$
18. (.75)(500 dozen) = 375 dozen purchased in 2000 at a cost of ($1.20)(1.20) = $1.44 per dozen. Total cost for 2000 = ($1.44) (375) = $540
19. Total time = 1 hour + 450/75 hrs. = 7 hours
20. (.30)(420) - (1/7)(420) = 126 - 60 = 66

21. Cost per minute = (120)(.02) = \$2.40. Then, \$12 ÷ \$2.40 = 5 minutes

22. (32)(22) ÷ 16 = 44 clerks

23. Total amount paid = (20)(\$27,500)(2/12) + (18)(\$31,500) (4/12) + (22)(\$30,000)(3/12) = \$445,666.$\overline{6}$ ≈ \$450,000

24. Number of accountants with college degrees and five years of experience = (2300)(.05)(.80)(1/2) = 46

25. Let x = regular hourly pay. Then, (8)(x) + (1)(1.5x) = \$1.71 So, 9.5x = 171. Solving, x = \$18

TEST 2

DIRECTIONS: Each question or incomplete statement is followed by several suggested answers or completions. Select the one that BEST answers the question or completes the statement. *PRINT THE LETTER OF THE CORRECT ANSWER IN THE SPACE AT THE RIGHT.*

1. Assume that you know the capacity of a filing cabinet, the extent of which it is filled, and the daily rate at which material is being added to the file. 1.____
   In order to estimate how many more days it will take for the cabinet to be filled to capacity, you should

   A. divide the extent to which the cabinet is filled by the daily rate
   B. take the difference between the capacity of the cabinet and the material in it, and multiply the result by the daily rate of adding material
   C. divide the daily rate of adding material by the difference between the capacity of the cabinet and the material in it
   D. take the difference between the capacity of the cabinet and the material in it, and divide the result by the daily rate of adding material

2. Suppose you have been asked to compute the average salary earned in your department during the past year. For each of the divisions of the department, you are given the number of employees and the average salary. 2.____
   In order to find the requested overall average salary for the department, you should

   A. add the average salaries of the various divisions and divide the total by the number of divisions
   B. multiply the number of employees in each division by the corresponding average salary, add the results and divide the total by the number of employees in the department
   C. add the average salaries of the various divisions and divide the total by the total number of employees in the department
   D. multiply the sum of the average salaries of the various divisions by the total number of divisions and divide the resulting product by the total number of employees in the department

3. Suppose that a group of six clerks has been assigned to assemble the duplicated pages of a report into completed copies. After four hours of work, they have been able to complete one-third of the job. 3.____
   In order to assemble all the remaining copies in three more hours of work, the number of clerks which will have to be added to the original six, assuming that all the clerks assigned to this task work at the same rate of speed, is

   A. 10 B. 16 C. 2 D. 6

4. A study of the grades of students in a certain college revealed that in 2005, 15% fewer students received a passing grade in mathematics than in 2004, whereas in 2006 the number of students passing mathematics increased 15% over 2005. 4.____
   On the basis of this study, it would be MOST accurate to conclude that

   A. the same percentage of students passed mathematics in 2004 as in 2006
   B. of the three years studied, the greatest percentage of students passed mathematics in 2006

C. the percentage of students who passed mathematics in 2006 was less than the percentage passing this subject in 2004
D. the percentage of students passing mathematics in 2004 was 15% greater than the percentage of students passing this subject in 2006

5. A city department employs 1,400 people, of whom 35% are clerks and 1/8 are stenographers. 5.____
The number of employees in the department who are neither clerks nor stenographers is

A. 640 B. 665 C. 735 D. 760

6. Assume that there are 190 papers to be filed and that Clerk A and Clerk B are assigned to file these papers. If Clerk A files 40 papers more than Clerk B, then the number of papers that Clerk A files is 6.____

A. 75 B. 110 C. 115 D. 150

7. A stock clerk had on hand the following items: 7.____
500 pads, each worth 16 cents
130 pencils, each worth 12 cents
50 dozen rubber bands, worth 8 cents a dozen
If, from this stock, he issued 125 pads, 45 pencils, and 48 rubber bands, the value of the remaining stock would be

A. $25.72 B. $27.80 C. $70.52 D. $73.88

8. In a particular agency, there were 160 accidents in 2002. Of these accidents, 75% were due to unsafe acts and the rest were due to unsafe conditions. In the following year, a special safety program was established. The number of accidents in 2004 due to unsafe acts was reduced to 35% of what it had been in 2002. 8.____
How many accidents due to unsafe acts were there in 2004?

A. 20 B. 36 C. 42 D. 56

9. At the end of every month, the petty cash fund of Agency A is reimbursed for payments made from the fund during the month. During the month of February, the amounts paid from the fund were entered on receipts as follows: 10 bus fares of $1.40 each and one taxi fare of $14.00. At the end of the month, the money left in the fund was in the following denominations: 60 one-dollar bills, 16 quarters, 40 dimes, and 80 nickels. 9.____
If the petty cash fund is reduced by 20% for the following month, how much money will there be available in the petty cash fund for March?

A. $44 B. $80 C. $86 D. $100

10. An employee worked on a job for 6 weeks, 5 days per week, and 8 hours per day. 10.____
How many hours did he work on the job?

A. 40 B. 48 C. 55 D. 240

11. Divide 35 by .7. 11.____

A. 5 B. 42 C. 50 D. 245

12. .1% of 25 = 12.____

A. .025 B. .25 C. 2.5 D. 25

13. In a city agency, 80 percent of the total number of employees are more than 25 years of age and 65 percent of the total number of employees are high school graduates. 13.____
The SMALLEST possible percent of employees who are both high school graduates and more than 25 years of age is

A. 35% B. 45% C. 55% D. 65%

14. Two clerical units, X and Y, each having a different number of clerks, are assigned to file registration cards. It takes Unit X, which contains 8 clerks, 21 days to file the same number of cards that Unit Y can file in 28 days. It is also a fact that Unit X can file 174,528 cards in 72 days. 14.____
Assuming that all the clerks in both units work at the same rate of speed, the number of cards which can be filed by Unit Y in 144 days, if 4 more clerks are added to the staff of Unit Y, is MOST NEARLY

A. 392,000 B. 436,000 C. 523,000 D. 669,000

15. Assume that two machines, each costing $14,750, were purchased for your office. Each machine requires the services of an operator at a salary of $2,000 per month. These machines are to replace six clerks, two of whom earn $1,550 per month each, and four of whom earn $1,700 per month each. 15.____
The number of months it will take for the cost of the machines to be made up from the savings in salaries is

A. less than four
B. four
C. five
D. more than five

16. Suppose that the amount of stationery used by your department in August decreased by 16% as compared with the amount used in July, and that the amount used in September increased by 25% as compared with the amount used in August. 16.____
The amount of stationery used in September as compared with the amount used in July is

A. greater by 5 percent
B. less by 5 percent
C. greater by 9 percent
D. the same

17. An employee earns $48 a day and works 5 days a week. 17.____
He will earn $2,160 in ______ weeks.

A. 5 B. 7 C. 8 D. 9

18. In a certain bureau, the entire staff consists of 1 senior supervisor, 2 supervisors, 6 assistant supervisors, and 54 associate workers. 18.____
The percent of the staff who are not associate workers is MOST NEARLY

A. 14 B. 21 C. 27 D. 32

19. In a certain bureau, five employees each earn $1,000 a month, another 3 employees each earn $2,200 a month, and another two employees each earn $1,400 a month. 19.____
The monthly payroll for these employees is

A. $3,600 B. $8,800 C. $11,400 D. $14,400

20. An employee contributes 5% of his salary to the pension fund. 20.____
If his salary is $1,200 a month, the amount of his contribution to the pension fund in a year is

A. $480 B. $720 C. $960 D. $1,200

21. The number of square feet in an area that is 50 feet long and 30 feet wide is 21.____

A. 80 B. 150 C. 800 D. 1,500

22. A farm hand was paid a weekly wage of $332.16 for a 48-hour work week. As a result of a new labor contract, he is paid $344.96 a week for a 44-hour work week with time and one-half pay for time worked in excess of 44 hours in any work week. 22.____
If he continues to work 48 hours weekly under the new contract, the amount by which his average hourly rate for a 48-hour work week under the new contract exceeds the hourly rate previously paid him lies between ______ and ______ cents, inclusive.

A. 91;100 B. 101;110 C. 111;120 D. 121;130

23. Each side of a square room, which is being used as an office, measures 66 feet. The floor of the room is divided by six traffic aisles, each aisle being six feet wide. Three of the aisles run parallel to the east and west sides of the room, and the other three run parallel to the north and south sides of the room, so that the remaining floor space is divided into 16 equal sections. If all of the floor space which is not being used for traffic aisles is occupied by desk and chair sets, and each set takes up 24 square feet of floor space, the number of desk and chair sets in the room is 23.____

A. 80 B. 64 C. 36 D. 96

24. In 2005, a city agency bought 12,000 envelopes at $4.00 per hundred. In 2006, the price of envelopes purchased was 40 percent higher than the 2005 price, but only 60 percent as many envelopes were bought. 24.____
The total cost of the envelopes purchased in 2006 was MOST NEARLY

A. $250 B. $320 C. $400 D. $480

25. In a city agency, 25 percent of the women employees and 50 percent of the men employees attended a general staff meeting. 25.____
If 48 percent of all the employees in the agency are women, the percentage of all the employees who attended the meeting is

A. 36% B. 37% C. 38% D. 75%

KEY (CORRECT ANSWERS)

1. D
2. B
3. A
4. C
5. C

6. C
7. D
8. C
9. B
10. D

11. C
12. A
13. B
14. A
15. C

16. A
17. D
18. A
19. D
20. B

21. D
22. D
23. D
24. C
25. C

SOLUTIONS TO PROBLEMS

1. To determine number of days required to fill cabinet to capacity, subtract material in it from capacity amount, then divide by daily rate of adding material. Example: A cabinet already has 10 folders in it, and the capacity is 100 folders. Suppose 5 folders per day are added. Number of days to fill to capacity = (100-10) ÷ 5 = 18

2. To determine overall average salary, multiply number of employees in each division by that division's average salary, add results, then divide by total number of employees. Example: Division A has 4 employees with average salary of $40,000; division B has 6 employees with average salary of $36,000; division C has 2 employees with average salary of $46,000. Average salary = [(4)($40,000)+(6)($36,000)+(2)($46,000)] / 12 = $39,000

3. (6)(4) = 24 clerk-hours. Since only one-third of work has been done, (24) (3) - 24 = 48 clerk-hours remain. Then, 48 3 = 16 clerks. Thus, 16 - 6 = 10 additional clerks.

4. The percentage of students passing math in 2006 was less than the percentage of those passing math in 2004. Example: Suppose 400 students passed math in 2004. Then, (400)(.85) = 340 passed in 2005. Finally, (340)(1.15) = 391 passed in 2006.

5. 1400 - (.35)(1400) - (1/8)(1400) = 735

6. Let x = number of papers filed by clerk A, x-40 = number of papers filed by clerk B. Then, x + (x-40) = 190 Solving, x = 115

7. (500-125)(.16) + (130-45)(.12) + (50 - 48/12)(.08) = $60.00 + $10.20 + $3.68 = $73.88

8. (160)(.75) = 120 accidents due to unsafe acts in 2002. In 2004, (120)(.35) = 42 accidents due to unsafe acts

9. Original amount at beginning of February in the fund = (10)($1.40) + (1)($14.00) + (60)($1) + (16)(.25) + (40)(.10) + (80)(.05) = $100. Finally, for March, ($100)(.80) = $80 will be available

10. Total hours = (6)(5)(8) = 240

11. 35 ÷ .7 = 50

12. .1% of 25 = (.001)(25) = .025

13. Let A = percent of employees who are at least 25 years old and B = percent of employees who are high school graduates. Also, let N = percent of employees who fit neither category and J = percent of employees who are in both categories.
Then, 100 = A + B + N - J. Substituting, 100 = 80 + 65 + N - J To minimize J, let N = 0. So, 100 = 80 + 65 + 0 - J. Solving, J = 45

14. Let Y = number of clerks in Unit Y. Then, (8)(21) = (4)(28), so Y = 6. Unit X has 8 clerks who can file 174,528 cards in 72 flays; thus, each clerk in Unit X can file 174,528 ÷ 72 ÷ 8 = 303 cards per day. Adding 4 clerks to Unit Y will yield 10 clerks in that unit. Since their rate is equal to that of Unit X, the clerks in Unit Y will file, in 144 days, is (303)(10)(144) = 436,320 ≈ 436,000 cards.

15. Let x = required number of months. The cost of the machines in x months = (2)(14,750) + (2)(2000)(x) = 29,500 + 4000x. The savings in salaries for the displaced clerks = x[(2)(1550) +(4)(1700)] = 9900x. Thus, 29,500 + 4000x = 9900x. Solving, x = 5. So, five months will elapse in order to achieve a savings in cost.

16. Let x = amount used in July, so that .84x = amount used in August. For September, the amount used = (.84x)(1.25) = 1.05x. This means the amount used in September is 5% more than the amount used in July.

17. Each week he earns ($48)(5) = $240. Then, $2160 ÷ $240 = 9 weeks

18. (1+2+6) ÷ 63 = 1/7 ≈ 14%

19. Monthly payroll = (5)($1000) + (3)($2200) + (2)($1400) = $14,400

20. Yearly contribution to pension fund = (12)($1200)(.05) = $720

21. (50')(30') = 1500 sq.ft.

22. Old rate = 332.16 ÷ 48 = 6.92 (48 hours)
New rate = 344.96 (44 hours)
Overtime rate = 344.96 ÷ 44 = 7.75/hr. x 1.5 x 4 = 46.48
344.96 + 46.48 = 391.44
391.44 ÷ 48 = 8.15
815 - 692 = 123 cents an hour more

23. Each of the 16 sections is a square with side [66'-(3)(6')] ÷ 4 = 12'. So each section contains (12')(12') = 144 sq.ft.
The number of desk and chair sets = (144 ÷ 24) (16) = 96

24. In 2006, (.60)(12,000) = 7200 envelopes were bought and the price per hundred was ($4.00)(1.40) = $5.60. The total cost = (5.60)(72) = $403.20 ≈ $400

25. (.25)(.48) + (.50)(.52) = .38 = 38%

TEST 3

DIRECTIONS: Each question or incomplete statement is followed by several suggested answers or completions. Select the one that BEST answers the question or completes the statement. *PRINT THE LETTER OF THE CORRECT ANSWER IN THE SPACE AT THE RIGHT.*

1. According to one suggested filing system, no more than 12 folders should be filed behind any one file guide and from 10 to 20 file guides should be used in each file drawer. Based on this filing system, the MAXIMUM number of folders that a four-drawer file cabinet can hold is 1.____

   A. 240 B. 480 C. 960 D. 1,200

2. A certain office uses three different forms. Last year, it used 3,500 copies of Form L, 6,700 copies of Form M, and 10,500 copies of Form P. This year, the office expects to decrease the use of each of these forms by 5%. The TOTAL number of these three forms which the office expects to use this year is 2.____

   A. 10,350 B. 16,560 C. 19,665 D. 21,735

3. The hourly rate of pay for a certain part-time employee is computed by dividing his yearly salary rate by the number of hours in the work year. The employee's yearly salary rate is $18,928, and there are 1,820 hours in the work year.
   If this employee works 18 hours during one week, his TOTAL earnings for these 18 hours are 3.____

   A. $180.00 B. $183.60 C. $187.20 D. $190.80

4. Assume that the regular work week of an employee is 35 hours and that the employee is paid for any extra hours worked according to the following schedule. For hours worked in excess of 35 hours, up to and including 40 hours, the employee receives his regular hourly rate of pay. For hours worked in excess of 40 hours, the employee receives 1 1/2 times his hourly rate of pay.
   If the employee's hourly rate of pay is $11.20 and he works 43 hours during a certain week, his TOTAL pay for the week would be 4.____

   A. $481.60 B. $498.40 C. $556.00 D. $722.40

5. A clerk divided his 35 hour work week as follows: 5.____
   1/5 of his time in sorting mail;
   1/2 of his time in filing letters; and
   1/7 of his time in reception work.
   The rest of his time was devoted to messenger work. The percentage of time spent on messenger work by the clerk during the week was MOST NEARLY

   A. 6% B. 10% C. 14% D. 16%

6. A city department has set up a computing unit and has rented 5 computing machines at a yearly rental of $700 per machine. In addition, the cost to the department for the maintenance and repair of each of these machines is $50 per year. Five computing machine operators, each receiving an annual salary of $15,000, and a supervisor, who receives $19,000 a year, have been assigned to this unit. This unit will perform the work previously performed by 10 employees whose combined salary was $162,000 a year.
   On the basis of these facts, the savings that will result from the operation of this computing unit for 5 years will be MOST NEARLY 6.____

   A. $250,000 B. $320,000 C. $330,000 D. $475,000

7. Twelve clerks are assigned to enter certain data on index cards. This number of clerks could perform the task in 18 days. After these clerks have worked on this assignment for 6 days, 4 more clerks are added to the staff to do this work.
Assuming that all the clerks work at the same rate of speed, the entire task, instead of taking 18 days, will be performed in _______ days. 7.____

A. 9 B. 12 C. 15 D. 16

8. Suppose that a file cabinet, which has a capacity of 3,000 cards, now contains approximately 2,200 cards. Cards are added to the file at the average rate of 30 cards a day.
To find the number of days it will take to fill the cabinet to capacity, 8.____

A. divide 3,000 by 30
B. divide 2,200 by 3,000
C. divide 800 by 30
D. multiply 30 by the fraction 2,200 divided by 3,000

9. Six gross of special drawing pencils were purchased for use in a city department.
If the pencils were used at the rate of 24 a week, the MAXIMUM number of weeks that the six gross of pencils would last is _______ weeks. 9.____

A. 6 B. 12 C. 24 D. 36

10. A stock clerk had 600 pads on hand. He then issued 3/8 of his supply of pads to Division X, 1/4 to Division Y, and 1/6 to Division Z.
The number of pads remaining in stock is 10.____

A. 48 B. 125 C. 240 D. 475

11. If a certain job can be performed by 18 clerks in 26 days, the number of clerks needed to perform the job in 12 days is _______ clerks. 11.____

A. 24 B. 30 C. 39 D. 52

12. In anticipation of a seasonal increase in the amount of work to be performed by his division, a division chief prepared the following list of additional temporary employees needed by his division and the amount of time they would be employed: 12.____

26 cashiers, each at $24,000 a year, for 2 months
15 laborers, each at $85.00 a day, for 50 days
6 clerks, each at $21,000 a year, for 3 months

The total approximate cost for this additional personnel would be MOST NEARLY

A. $200,000 B. $250,000 C. $500,000 D. $600,000

13. A copy machine company offered to sell a city agency 4 copy machines at a discount of 15% from the list price, and to allow the agency $850 for each of its two old machines.
The list price of the new machines is $6,250 per machine.
If the city agency accepts this offer, the amount of money it will have to provide for the purchase of these 4 machines is 13.____

A. $17,350 B. $22,950 C. $19,550 D. $18,360

14. A stationery buyer was offered bond paper at the following price scale: 14.____
    $1.43 per ream for the first 1,000 reams
    $1.30 per ream for the next 4,000 reams
    $1.20 per ream for each additional ream beyond 5,000 reams
    If the buyer ordered 10,000 reams of paper, the average cost per ream, computed to the nearest cent, was

    A. $1.24 B. $1.26 C. $1.31 D. $1.36

15. A clerk has 5.70 percent of his salary deducted for his retirement pension. 15.____
    If this clerk's annual salary is $20,400, the monthly deduction for his retirement pension is

    A. $298.20 B. $357.90 C. $1,162.80 D. $96.90

16. In a certain bureau, two-thirds of the employees are clerks and the remainder are typists. 16.____
    If there are 90 clerks, then the number of typists in this bureau is

    A. 135 B. 45 C. 120 D. 30

17. The number of investigations conducted by an agency in 1999 was 3,600. In 2000, the number of investigations conducted was one-third more than in 1999. The number of investigations conducted in 2001 was three-fourths of the number conducted in 2000. It is anticipated that the number of investigations conducted in 2002 will be equal to the average of the three preceding years. On the basis of this information, the MOST accurate of the following statements is that the number of investigations conducted in 17.____

    A. 1999 is larger than the number anticipated for 2002
    B. 2000 is smaller than the number anticipated for 2002
    C. 2001 is equal to the number conducted in 1999
    D. 2001 is larger than the number anticipated in 2002

18. A city agency engaged in repair work uses a small part which the city purchases for 14 each. Assume that, in a certain year, the total expenditure of the city for this part was $700. 18.____
    How many of these parts were purchased that year?

    A. 50 B. 200 C. 2,000 D. 5,000

19. The work unit which you supervise is responsible for processing 15 reports per month. 19.____
    If your unit has 4 clerks and the best worker completes 40% of the reports himself, how many reports would each of the other clerks have to complete if they all do an equal number?

    A. 1 B. 2 C. 3 D. 4

20. Assume that the work unit in which you work has 24 clerks and 18 stenographers. In order to change the ratio of stenographers to clerks so that there is 1 stenographer for every 4 clerks, it would be necessary to REDUCE the number of stenographers by 20.____

A. 3 B. 6 C. 9 D. 12

21. The arithmetic mean salary for five employees earning $18,500, $18,300, $18,600, $18,400, and $18,500, respectively, is 21.____

A. $18,450 B. $18,460 C. $18,475 D. $18,500

22. Last year, a city department which is responsible for purchasing supplies ordered bond paper in equal quantities from 22 different companies. The price was exactly the same for each company, and the total cost for the 22 orders was $693,113.
Assuming prices did not change during the year, the cost of each order was MOST NEARLY 22.____

A. $31,490 B. $31,495 C. $31,500 D. $31,505

23. Suppose that a large bureau has 187 employees. On a particular day, approximately 14% of these employees are not available for work because of absences due to vacation, illness, or other reasons. Of the remaining employees, 1/7 are assigned to a special project while the balance are assigned to the normal work of the bureau. The number of employees assigned to the normal work of the bureau on that day is 23.____

A. 112 B. 124 C. 138 D. 142

24. Suppose that you are in charge of a typing pool of 8 typists. Two typists type at the rate of 38 words per minute; three type at the rate of 40 words per minute; three type at the rate of 42 words per minute. The average typewritten page consists of 50 lines, 12 words per line. Each employee works from 9 to 5 with one hour off for lunch.
The total number of pages typed by this pool in one day is, on the average, CLOSEST to _______ pages. 24.____

A. 205 B. 225 C. 250 D. 275

25. Suppose that part-time workers are paid $7.20 an hour, prorated to the nearest half hour, with pay guaranteed for a minimum of four hours if services are required for less than four hours. In one operation, part-time workers signed the time sheet as follows: 25.____

Worker	In	Out
A	8:00 A.M.	11:35 A.M.
B	8:30 A.M.	3:20 P.M.
C	7:55 A.M.	11:00 A.M.
D	8:30 A.M.	2:25 P.M.

How much would TOTAL payment to these part-time workers amount to for this operation, assuming that those who stayed after 12 Noon were not paid for one hour which they took off for lunch?

A. $134.40 B. $136.80 C. $142.20 D. $148.80

KEY (CORRECT ANSWERS)

1. C
2. C
3. C
4. B
5. D

6. B
7. C
8. C
9. D
10. B

11. C
12. A
13. C
14. B
15. D

16. B
17. C
18. D
19. C
20. D

21. B
22. D
23. C
24. B
25. B

SOLUTIONS TO PROBLEMS

1. Maximum number of folders = (4)(12)(20) = 960

2. (3500+6700+10,500)(.95) = 19,665

3. Hourly rate = $18,928 ÷ 1820 = $10.40. Then, the pay for 18 hours = ($10.40)(18) = $187.20

4. Total pay = ($11.20)(40) + ($11.20)(1.5)(3) = $498.40

5. (1 - 1/5 - 1/2 - 1/7)(100)% ≈ 16%

6. Previous cost for five years = ($324,000)(5) = $1,620,000
   Present cost for five years = (5)(5)($1,400) + (5)(5)($100) + (5)(5)($30,000) + (1)(5)($38,000) = $977,500 The net savings = $642,500 ≈ $640,000

7. (12)(18) = 216 clerk-days. Then, 216 - (12)(6) = 144 clerk-days of work left when 4 more clerks are added. Now, 16 clerks will finish the task in 144 ÷ 16 = 9 more days. Finally, the task will require a total of 6 + 9 = 15 days.

8. Number of days needed = (3000-2200) ÷ 30 = 26.7, which is equivalent to dividing 800 by 30.

9. (6)(144) = 864 pencils purchased. Then, 864 ÷ 24 = 36 maximum number of weeks

10. Number of remaining pads = 600 - (1)(600) - (1/4)(600) - (1/6)(600) = 125

11. (18)(26) ÷ 12 = 39 clerks

12. Total cost = (26)($24,000)(2/12) + (15)($85)(50) + (6)($21,000)(3/12) = $199,250 $200,000

13. (4)($6250)(.85) - (2)($850) = $19,550

14. Total cost = ($1.43)(1000) + ($1.30)(4000) + ($1.20X5000) = $12,630. Average cost per ream = $12,630 10,000 ≈ $1.26

15. Monthly salary = $20,400 ÷ 12 = $1700. Thus, the monthly deduction for his pension = ($1700)(.057) + $96.90

16. Number of employees = 90 ÷ 2/3 = 135. Then, the number of typists = (1/3)(135) = 45

17. The number of investigations for each year is as follows:
    1999: 3600
    2000: (3600)(1 1/3) = 4800
    2001: (4800)(3/4) = 3600
    2002: (3600+4800+3600)/3 = 4000
    So, the number of investigations were equal for 1999 and 2001.

18. $700 ÷ .14 = 5000 parts

19. The best worker does (.40)(15) = 6 reports. The other 9 reports are divided equally among the other 3 clerks, so each clerk does 9 ÷ 3 = 3 reports.

20. 1:4 = 6:24 . Thus, the number of stenographers must be reduced by 18 - 6 = 12

21. Mean = ($18,500+$18,300+$18,400+$18,500) ÷ 5 = $18,460

22. The cost per order = $693,113 ÷ 22 ≈ $31,505

23. 187 - (.14) = 26. 187 - 26 = 161 - 1/7 (161) = 23
161 - 23 = 138

24. Number of words typed in 1 min. = (2)(38) + (3)(40) + (3)(42) = 322. For 7 hours, the total number of words typed = (7)(60)(322) = 135,240. Each page contains (on the average) (50)(12) = 600 words. Finally, 135,240 ÷ 600 ≈ 225 pages

25. Worker A = ($7.20)(4) = $28.80
Worker B = ($7.20)(3 1/2) + ($7.20)(2 1/2) = $43.20
Worker C = ($7.20)(4) = $28.80
Worker D = ($7.20)(3 1/2) + ($7.20)(1 1/2) = $36.00
Total for all 4 workers = $136.80
Note: Workers A and C received the guaranteed minimum 4 hours pay each.